W9-CNR-330

DONAU

IMPRESSUM

Die Deutsche Bibliothek – CIP-Einheitsaufnahme

Donau: Fotoessay / Inge Morath. Mit einem Text von Karl-Markus Gauß. - Salzburg ; Wien : Müller, 1995

(Edition Fotohof ; Bd. 13)

ISBN 3-7013-0916-7

NE: Morath, Inge; Gauß, Karl-Markus; GT

Edition Fotohof

Herausgegeben von/ published by Kurt Kaindl

Band 13: Donau / Volume 13: The Danube

Umschlaggestaltung unter Verwendung eines Fotos von Inge Morath, 1994.

Cover design with photograph by Inge Morath, 1994.

Übersetzung des Textes von Karl-Markus Gauß durch Mary B. Murrow und Tom Appleton, Wien.

The text by Karl-Markus Gauß was translated by Mary B. Murrow and Tom Appleton, Vienna.

Vergrößerungen der Originalnegative unter Aufsicht von Inge Morath durch Andrew Phelps.

Enlargements were made from the original negatives by Andrew Phelps, under the supervision of Inge Morath.

Die Bildunterschriften stammen von Inge Morath.

Captions by Inge Morath.

Gefördert durch das Bundesministerium für Wissenschaft, Forschung und Kunst.

Supported by the Austrian Ministry of Education, Science and Art.

Produktion / Production: Kaindl EVG & Kanzlei mit Vision

Produktionsteam / Production team: Brigitte Blüml, Sigrid Dornetshuber, Kurt Kaindl, Andrew Phelps

Lektorat / Publisher's reader: Christa Gürtler

Gestaltung / Design: Kanzlei mit Vision

Lithos / Lithographs: Repro Atelier Reinhold Czerlinka, Grödig

Druck / Printing: Landesverlag, Linz

Printed in Austria

ISBN 3-7013-0916-7

© 1995 Otto Müller Verlag Salzburg/Wien und bei den Autoren

© der Fotografien by Inge Morath, Magnum Photos

Alle Rechte vorbehalten

DONAU

Inge Morath

Mit einem Essay von Karl-Markus Gauß

Inge Morath

1995

Edition Fotohof im Otto Müller Verlag

GEWIDMET
ARTHUR UND REBECCA.
BRIGITTE UND KURT, MEINEN REISEBEGLEITERN

DEDICATED TO
ARTHUR UND REBECCA.
BRIGITTE AND KURT, MY TRAVEL COMPANIONS

DIE LEHRE DER DONAU

Karl-Markus Gauß

DER EXPERIMENTELLE FLUSS

Ein belgischer Ingenieur namens Maire hatte im 18. Jahrhundert eine kühne Vision. Er sah Europa, wie es von den Zufällen der Geographie beherrscht wurde, von unverschiebbaren Gebirgszügen, unvernünftig leeren Ebenen, mächtigen, doch kaum genutzten Flüssen, und dachte, daß es nicht gut war. Der kühle Phantast ahnte ein anderes Europa und machte sich auf nach Wien, den Kaiser für seinen Traum zu begeistern. Und Josef II., Habsburgs freiester Geist und mutigster Reformer auf dem Herrscherthron, sah gleich seinem Ingenieur, daß es vieles gab, das zu verbessern war. Im einzelnen zu durchdenken, wie Wien zum Zentrum eines ganz Europa erfassenden Systems von Wasserstraßen werden könnte, war nun der Auftrag, mit dem Maire zu zeichnen, zu berechnen begann und zu träumen, die Unvollkommenheiten der Natur zu berichtigen fort-

fuhr. Die Donau, der europäische Strom, sollte zum Strom Europas werden, an den die anderen bedeutenden Flüsse über eine Vielzahl von Kanälen angeschlossen würden, sodaß von überall die Meere, die den Kontinent umspülten, auf dem Wasser zu erreichen wären. Mit Etsch und Adria im Süden, im Westen mit Main und Rhein, mit der tschechischen Moldau, der polnischen Weichsel, dem Dnjestr im fernen Zarenreich galt es die Donau über ein feines Netz von Kanälen, Durchstichen, künstlichen Wasserwegen zu verbinden. Aus den Plänen Maires, so leidenschaftlich entworfen, wurde damals nicht viel, und noch heute mögen sich manche dem belgischen Ingenieur hinterherärgern, daß zwischen Österreich und dem Mittelmeer störend wie je die Alpen ragen, von keinem Kanal durchstoßen. Doch selbst aus ihrem Scheitern geht hervor, daß der Kaiser und sein Landverbesserer ein Europa bauen wollten, das im Zeichen der Donau stand. Geblieben ist uns

davon immerhin die Gewißheit, daß die Donau alles kennt, was Europa kennt. Nichts Neues ereignet sich, es sei denn, an der Donau würde es erprobt werden, und nichts Altes kann verschwinden noch aus glücklicher Vergessenheit wieder auftauchen, das nicht schon in der Donau versunken war oder gespenstisch wieder an eines ihrer Ufer trat. Ungezählte Nationalitäten haben an diesem mächtigen Strom gesiedelt, der alles gesehen und erlitten hat, was die mittel- und südosteuropäischen Völker zuwegegebracht oder sich und einander angetan haben. Wovor uns heute schaudert, vor der Grimasse des Chauvinismus, dem Haß der aufeinander angewiesenen, doch periodisch aufeinander gehetzten Völker, dem Fanatismus der Enge, vor der Zerstörung der Natur, dem einebnenden Tritt des Fortschritts — dies alles finden wir an der Donau, verheerender denn irgendwo. Mit dem Schrecken findet sich an der Donau aber auch, was uns auf der Welt fas-

DEUTSCHLAND. DONAUESCHINGEN. 1995.
GERMANY. DONAUESCHINGEN. 1995.

ziniert: die Schönheit einer bald lieblichen, bald schroffen, oft überraschenden Landschaft; der Reichtum an Kultur, die Vielfalt an Lebensweisen, die einander unaufhörlich beeinflussen und bereichern, nicht übertrumpfen; heiter gelassene Kunst und leidenschaftliche Lust des Lebens, oft bewiesener Großmut der Menschen; ihre trotzige Kraft, wider die Vereinheitlichung das Besondere zu entfalten und auf dem zu beharren, was sie unterscheidet . . . Die Donau hat die schlimmsten Despoten

gekannt, aber auch gesehen, wie sie sich mit ihren Lakaien überstürzt davonstehlen mußten; an der Donau ist viel Blut geflossen, vergossen für Besitz, Herrschaft, Ideologie, doch an der Donau ist auch immer wieder die Toleranz wirksam geworden, nicht als intellektuelle Utopie aufgeklärter Geister oder als politisches Programm wohlmeinender Staatsdenker, sondern als lebensnahes Prinzip des Alltags, als praktizierte Lebensweisheit der sogenannten gewöhnlichen Menschen.

Es ist ein grauenhaftes und rätselhaftes Phänomen, daß die Donau nicht nur Romantiker und Naturfreunde, Abenteurer, Verliebte, Händler, Fischer angezogen hat, sondern auch Mörder, die für ihre Verbrechen die Ufer der Donau suchten. In jedem Krieg, der in einem der Donauländer geführt wurde, sind Menschen aus dem Landesinneren an die Donau gebracht worden, einzig zum Zwecke, daß ihnen dort ein schreckliches Ende bereitet werde. Im Jänner 1942 wird in der Hauptstadt der Wojwodina, in der von urdenklichen Zeiten her viele Nationalitäten friedlich nebeneinander und miteinander leben, die berüchtigte Razzia von Novi Sad exekutiert. Die Juden und Hunderte Serben der Stadt werden in einem langen, stundenlang immer wieder stockenden Elendszug an den zugefrorenen Fluß geführt, wo sie von Einheiten der ungarischen Besatzer erschossen und durch ausgesägte Löcher in die Donau gestoßen werden. Ähnliche Massaker sollten in Baja und in Budapest folgen, wo für die entsetzlichsten, keineswegs spontanen, sondern von langer Hand vorbereiteten Gewalttaten stets die Donauufer als Schauplatz gewählt wurden, als würden so die Verbrechen aus dem Gedächtnis fortgeschwemmt werden. Die Wojwodina, die fruchtbare Ebene zwischen Donau, Theiß und Save, war eine europäische Versuchsstation, in der das Zusammenleben so vieler Nationen und Religionen exemplarisch erprobt wurde, zum Nutzen eines Landstrichs und seiner vielsprachigen Bewohner. Mit den unerhörten Verbrechen an der jüdischen und der serbischen Bevölkerung ist ein Experiment blutig zunichte gemacht worden, dessen Schlußakte mit der Austreibung der deutschsprachigen Bevölkerung besiegelt wurde, die doch 200 Jahre lang dort gelebt hatte und ganz zu unrecht für die Verbrechen büßen sollte, die im Namen Großdeutschlands verübt worden waren. Einst ein blühendes Land, Kornkammer vieler Völker und Speicher widerstreitender kultureller Erfahrungen, ist die Wojwodina nach dem Zweiten Weltkrieg, der sie zuerst um die Juden, die in die Vernichtung getrieben, und dann um die Donauschwaben, die außer Landes gejagt wurden, ärmer gemacht hatte, auch wirtschaftlich verarmt; freilich ist sie immer noch wohlhabend gewesen im Vergleich zu anderen Regionen der Föderativen Volksrepublik Jugoslawien, denn Tito hatte der Wojwodina den privilegierten Status einer autonomen Provinz innerhalb der Republik Serbien gesichert, welcher die Reste der alten Multinationalität schützen sollte; erst seitdem seine Nachfolger diesen Status beseitigt, die Wojwodina als bedrohtes Kernland des wahren Serbentums entdeckt und als Truppenübungsplatz des großserbischen Chauvinismus mißbraucht haben, ist sie wirklich darniedergekommen: was vordem wie von selber getan wurde, läßt sich heute durch keinerlei Kommandowirtschaft und auch nicht durch den nationalistischen Appell mehr mobilisieren. Ein Gebiet, das einst Serben, Ungarn, Juden, Schwaben, auch zahlenmäßig keineswegs unerheblichen Gruppen von Kroaten, Rumänen, Ukrainern, Slowaken, Bulgaren und selbst den, allerdings niemals für gleichberechtigt genommenen, Roma vielfältige Möglichkeiten der Entfaltung bot, ist endlich zur völkisch bereinigten Zone erklärt worden. Doch dieses Land wehrt sich, nimmt die neue, ihm unangemessene Ideologie nicht an — und verfällt. Es mehren sich die Nachrichten, daß das Wissen um ihre wahre Lebensgrundlage in dieser Region zunimmt und viele untergründig, doch alltäglich dem verordneten Prozeß der brutalen wie lebensfremden Gleichschaltung widerstehen. Und wie mit der Wojwodina, die stets bedroht war, in die Barbarei der Einfalt zu stürzen, und der doch immer wieder Menschen entwachsen, die den ganzen, den ungeteilten Reichtum dieser Region in sich tragen, wie mit der Wojwodina ist es mit der Slowakei, deren Hauptstadt drei Namen, Bratislava Preßburg Pozsony, und noch mehr Nationalitäten hat, ist es überall am Strom Europas: die Donau selber ist ein Experiment, das die ganze Welt betrifft — was hier mißrät, kann überall scheitern, was hier gelingt, läßt auch für anderswo hoffen.

DER STATISTISCHE FLUSS

Schon die antiken Geschichtsschreiber Ptolemäus, Strabon, Plinius suchten, was zu ihrer Zeit über die Donau bekannt war, zu sammeln und zu sichten. Heute hat sich die Donau-Forschung in aberdutzende Disziplinen ausgefächert, und unüberschaubar wächst die gelehrte Kenntnis eines Flusses, der unter jedem erdenklichen Gesichtspunkt untersucht, vermessen, erfaßt wird. Wer sich für "Keltische Höhensiedlungen an der mittleren Donau" interessiert, wird in besseren Bibliotheken so rasch fündig werden wie der, dem es um die "Geschichte und Technik der Fähren und Brücken über die österreichische Donau" geht; die ökologischen Wissenschaften stellen sich alljährlich warnend mit Forschungsberichten über "Naßbaggerungen im Landschaftsschutzgebiet" oder "Strategies for Conservation of a Danubian Fish Fauna" ein, Schriften, die so beachtet zu werden verdienten wie die auflagenstarken Radwanderführer, die saisonal aktualisiert werden und schon nach Dutzenden rechnen . . . Neben der spezialisierten Forschung, wie sie zuletzt in dem beachtlichen Katalog zur oberösterreichischen Landesausstellung 1994, "Facetten eines europäischen Stromes", erschöpfend dargetan wurde, wachsen freilich auch die Schwemmbänke, an denen sich die Donau-Feuilletonistik ablagert, und vor so viel gelehrten wie geschwätzigen Schriften reift unabweislich die Sorge: Gibt es sie wirklich, die Donau, oder ist sie eine Erfindung?

Vorweg sei daher kurz nacherzählt, was hinter Legenden und Mythen verborgen liegt, doch zweifelsfrei geschehen ist. Wie immer waren die Dinge am Anfang noch einfach: "Mit dem Zurückweichen des perialpinen Meeres, des Paratethys, zur Zeit der Unteren Süßwassermolasse, an der Wende vom Oligozän zum Miozän aus dem schweizerischen und westbayrischen Molasseland, nimmt die Geschichte der Donau ihren Anfang." Der Wissenschaftler Bernhard Gruber, von dem dieses schöne Stück Donauprosa stammt, setzt den Beginn unserer heutigen Donau — im Unterschied zur "Prädonau", jenem riesigen, langsam ostwärts strömenden System von Flüssen, Seen, Tümpeln — ungefähr bei elf Millionen Jahren vor unserer Zeit an. Diese elf Millionen Jahre mußten fast zur Gänze vergehen, bis der erste Mensch die Donau erreichte. Für einen echten Österreicher, reinblütigen Serben oder sonstwie purifizierten Nationalisten der Urzeit sollte man ihn nicht halten, der da irgendwann in der jüngsten Eiszeit, welche die Praehistoriker als Würm bezeichnen und beiläufig auf die hunderttausend Jahre zwischen 120.000

und 12.000 vor Christus schätzen, aus dem Dunkel der Geschichtslosigkeit auftauchte. Ins Dunkel, aus dem sie kamen, sollten ganze Völkerschaften wieder verschwinden, die zur Donau vorgestoßen waren und ein paar Jahre oder Jahrhunderte an ihren Ufern siedelten, um prächtige Goldschmiedearbeiten, Gräberfelder oder nichts als ihre magischen Namen zu hinterlassen, Petschenegen, Kumanen, Jazygen, Chasaren, die kunstreichen Awaren, die mächtigen Daker . . .

Obwohl über ihre beiden Quellen Breg und Brigach im Schwarzwald und ihre dritte in Donaueschingen ewig der Inkalpatriotische Streit gegangen und auch nicht präzise festzulegen ist, wo sie, im fast schon stehenden Gewässer des riesigen Donaudeltas, eigentlich ins Schwarze Meer mündet, wissen die Geographen heute seltsamerweise genau, daß die Donau eine Strecke von 2888 Kilometer zurücklegt, was sie nach der Wolga zum zweitlängsten Fluß Europas macht. Ein absolutes Gefälle von 678 Metern ermöglicht ihr ein meist sanftes, streckenweise indes wildes Fließen, ein Sachverhalt, der im statistischen Mittelwert von

23,53 Zentimetern Gefälle je Kilometer nur unvollkommenen Ausdruck findet. Ist sie bei Ulm mit einer Breite von etwa vierzig Metern noch ein deutscher Provinzfluß, hat sie sich bis Turnu Severin an der rumänisch-serbischen Grenze zu einem mächtigen Strom von 1300 Metern verbreitert. Erreicht sie bei Wien mit an die acht Kilometer in der Stunde eine vergleichsweise hohe Geschwindigkeit, ist sie im Donaudelta mit seinen unzähligen Seitenarmen und dem fließenden wie zurückfließenden Übergang ins Meer beinahe zum Stillstand gekommen. Den Fischreichtum der Donau rühmte in der Antike schon Plinius, der vom Hausen schwärmte, einem Fisch, der es auf neun Meter bringen konnte, und im Mittelalter noch Albertus Magnus in seinem Kompendium "De animalibus"; daß der Wiener Fischmarkt einst über fünfzig Fischarten anzubieten hatte, ist in den Berichten von staunenden Reisenden der frühen Neuzeit nachzulesen, indes der von alters her angesehene Beruf des Donaufischers vielerorts, und vor allem am reicheren Oberlauf, im 20. Jahrhundert ausgestorben ist, weswegen für die zahllosen Angler, die sich dort an den Ufern wei-

terhin tummeln, der Begriff des Sportfischers in Verwendung kommen mußte. Die Donauschiffahrt reicht in die älteste Zeit zurück, wobei anfangs bevorzugt flußnahe Rohstoffe

ÖSTERREICH. BEI WIEN. 1958.
AUSTRIA. NEAR VIENNA. 1958.

und Güter wie Holz, Wein, Erze transportiert wurden. Mit der Schiffahrt blühten die Ansiedlungen längs des Flusses und die edlen Künste des Schiffsbaus auf, denen über Jahrhunderte nicht nur einzelne Handwerksfamilien, sondern ganze Städtchen ihren Wohlstand verdankten. Im niederösterreichischen Persenbeug verließen schon um 1800 jedes Monat vier Schiffe eine frühindustrielle Reederei. Fast ebenso alt wie Schiffahrt und Schiffsbau sind die Versuche, beiden Gefahren Herr zu

werden, die dem geregelten Austausch von Waren auf der Donau drohten: den Tücken des Flusses suchte man durch kleinere und größere Regulierungen beizukommen und den

Wechselfällen der Politik durch Konventionen, die den Schiffsverkehr auch im Krisenfall nach zuverlässigen und festen Regeln garantieren sollten. Bis ins 19. Jahrhundert aber hatten die Schiffer Stromschnellen, Strudel, jähe Verengungen zu fürchten, etwa bei Grein im österreichischen Strudengau, der das Grauen der Schiffer im Namen trägt, oder vor der einzigartigen, imposanten Naturkulisse des Eisernen Tores, wo Balkan und Karpaten aufeinanderstoßen; über manchen

Konflikt und die erbitterte Feindschaft von Staaten und politischen Systemen hinaus blieben andrerseits zumeist Regeln in Kraft, wie sie selbst mitten im Kalten Krieg mit einer Konvention über die Schiffahrt auf der Donau festgeschrieben wurden, um die allgemeine Nutzung der Wasserstraße und die Internationalität des Flusses zu sichern. In den vierzig Jahren zwischen 1950 und 1990 hat sich denn die Tonnage der auf der Donau transportierten Waren, Rohstoffe und Güter immerhin verachtfacht. Durch den Rhein-Main-Donaukanal mit seinen Anschlüssen ist die europäische Kanalvernetzung, von der schon im 18. Jahrhundert der Kaiser und sein Ingenieur träumten, gegen Norden hin Wirklichkeit geworden. Der folgenreiche Bau von Kraftwerken — allein in Bayern sind zuletzt zwanzig davon errichtet worden — und die exzessive industrielle Nutzung des Flusses haben die Donau in den vergangenen Jahrzehnten ökologisch schwer geschädigt und den Artenreichtum drastisch reduziert. Der bedrohte Fluß ist andrerseits in allen seinen Ländern von Menschen wiederentdeckt worden, denen erst seine reale Gefährdung vor Augen führte, was er

seit jeher für das Leben ihres Gebietes bedeutete und daß es keine Gewähr dauernden Wohlstands für sie ist, wenn auch weiterhin bedenkenlos Gift und Abwässer in ihn geschüttet werden. Freilich, immer noch bietet die Donau Aulandschaften, weitausgedehnt und unberührt, wie sie auf diesem dichtbesiedelten Erdteil sonst kaum mehr zu finden sind. Selbst ein Theodor W. Adorno fiel, merklich ergriffen von dem Erlebnis der Natur, in den Ton raunender Beschwörung, als er im aufgeregten Jahr 1967 in die Donauauen bei Wien geführt wurde: "Rätselhaft die große Einsamkeit am Strom, nur wenige Kilometer von Wien. Von Landschaft und Flora, hier schon östlich, hält ein pußtahafter Bann die Menschen fern, als wollte der ins Unendliche offene Raum nicht gestört werden."

DER
ÜBERNATIONALE FLUSS

Wäre jener Ingenieur Maire auf eine abenteuerliche Reise gegangen, von der Quelle zur Mündung der Donau, er hätte etliche Länder passiert, Dutzende Sprachen gehört, nach vielen Riten beten können, aber auf seinen Wegen entlang des Stro-

mes nur einmal eine Grenze zu passieren gehabt. Der Oberlauf der Donau gehörte dem Kaiser, der Unterlauf dem Sultan. An deren jahrhundertelangen Kampf erinnert noch heute manches selbst in den abgelegenen Dörfern des Hinterlandes und natürlich in den Städten am Fluß. An vielen Orten ist so jener Grimm nie erlahmt, mit dem am Portal der Pfarrkirche St. Stephan in Tulln an der Donau ein österreichischer Doppeladler seit Jahrhunderten einen Türkenschädel in seinen Krallen hält. Seit damals, als Österreich sich zur Donau-Monarchie entfaltete und das Osmanische Reich seine europäischen Bastionen noch nicht preisgeben mochte, sind es erheblich mehr Staaten geworden, die von der Donau durchflossen werden. Immerhin zehn waren es bei der letzten Zählung — auf mehr bringt es kein anderer Fluß dieser Erde, und wäre er, wie der Jangtsekiang, Nil, Mississippi oder Amazonas, mehr als doppelt so lang wie die Donau. Zehn Staaten? Nimmt man zu Deutschland, Österreich, Ungarn, Rumänien und Bulgarien noch die jüngst entstandene Slowakei, die aus dem Zerfall Jugoslawiens hervorgegangenen Republiken Kroatien und Serbien und die

aus der Konkursmasse der Sowjetunion gebildeten Länder Ukraine und Moldawien dazu, steht man bei zehn. Doch könnten unberufen auch fünfzehn daraus werden, und noch mit zwanzig Donau-Staaten würden die neuen Herren der immer kleineren und immer patriotischeren Staaten jenes Ziel nicht erreicht haben, von dem sie alle träumen: ethnisch einheitliche, völkisch gereinigte Staatsgebilde, in denen jeweils einer einzigen Staatsnation die unerhörte Glückseligkeit beschieden wäre, mit nur einer geheiligten Sprache, einer allein seligmachenden Religion, einem volkstümlichen Despoten und einer einzigen vorbildlichen Dummheit ganz alleine unter sich leben zu dürfen.

D as Land an der Donau selbst, durch Geschichte so geformt wie durch die Natur, widerspricht der Zwangsvorstellung eines Kontinents, der aus lauter Nationalstaaten gebildet wird. Über Jahrhunderte waren die Völkerschaften, Nationalitäten und Religionsgemeinschaften auf der Donau und der Donau entlang in Bewegung gewesen. Auf Schiffen, deren menschliche Fracht oft in die Tiefe gerissen wurde, auf Pfer-

dewagen, die durch verseuchtes Gebiet fuhren, zu Fuß im Trott von Legionären und Söldnern; auf der Flucht vor religiöser Verfolgung, getrieben von der Sehnsucht nach eigenem Land, von den Mächtigen in die Fremde geschickt oder verlockt — in den Ländern der Donau waren die Menschen immer unterwegs, und wenn sie sich glücklich irgendwo seßhaft machten und eine Ansiedlung gründeten, wohnten schon im nächsten Dorf Menschen, die ihnen gleich waren nicht in Sprache und Ritus, aber im Schicksal: von irgendwoher verschlagen, voller Hoffnung, ihren Platz auf der Erde gefunden zu haben, an dem sie bleiben, arbeiten, sich vermehren und den Ihrigen einigen Wohlstand auf fruchtbarem Boden erwerben konnten. Gänzlich untrennbar sind die Nationalitäten im Donauraum ineinander verflochten, und wo einer herkommt, wie seine Großeltern sprachen, in welchem Gotteshaus wiederum deren Eltern ihre Gebete aufsagten, ist da zumeist durch keine Ahnenforschung mehr zu belegen. Überall an der Donau finden sich deutschsprachige Schwaben, die auf den ungarischen Namen Toth oder den slowakischen Prajko hören, indes ihre kroatischen Nachbarn den deutschen Namen Majster führen, die Ungarn gut serbisch Vidović heißen, die Rumänen sich gelegentlich slowakisch schreiben, und die Juden, am völkerverbindenden Fluß einst zwischen den Völkern so etwas wie die verbindende Nationalität, ihre Namen in vielerlei Sprachen führten und doch zu hüten wußten . . . und natürlich gibt es da eben nicht bloß, was zu erwarten wäre, nämlich katholische Kroaten und orthodoxe Serben, sondern auch noch Schokatzen und Bunjewatzen, die sich als Serben fühlen, aber katholischen Glaubens sind, und Pomaken, Bulgaren zwar, aber nicht nach bulgarisch orthodoxem Ritus, sondern islamisierte und darum bald privilegierte, bald mißachtete Bulgaren, und fromme Lippowaner, die aus den innersten Ländern ihrer strengen Glaubenstreue wegen ans Schwarze Meer kamen, aus der russischen Steppe und dem Staub Galiziens, und heute die Deltafischerei fast unter sich bestreiten . . . und unzählige anderer Menschen, die in Sprache, Religion, Gebräuchen nicht der einen, nicht der anderen, sondern gleich zwei, drei Nationalitäten zugleich zugehören, und wehe, wenn die Zeiten unerwartet

wiederkehren, da von einem jeden die Entscheidung nur für eine davon verlangt wird, wo es doch seine Identität ausmacht, daß diese durch solche Entscheidung zerrissen wird . . . Die nationale Identität, sie ist zumal am Balkan in vielen Fällen durchaus ungewiß, und vielleicht wird sie gerade deswegen manchesmal so martialisch betont, weil sie im Donauraum etwas Fließendes ist, keine zuverlässige Begrenzung hat. Der Haß auf den Nachbarn, wie er wiederkehrend politisch mobilisiert zu werden pflegt, ist auch ein Selbsthaß, der gegen die Unsicherheit, das Ungewisse, Fließende, Schwankende der eigenen Existenz gerichtet ist . . . So barbarisch könnten die ethnischen Säuberungen der Gegenwart und Zukunft jedoch gar nicht durchgeführt werden, daß im Donauraum je Nationalstaaten entstünden, die in ihren Grenzen nicht gleich mehrere, von uralten Zeiten eingesessene Ethnien, Minderheiten genannt, zu fassen hätten. Wenn der Wahn völkischer Reinheit bleckend aufstampft, rast er alsbald gegen jene Menschen, in denen das Erbe verschiedener Völker am schönsten gemischt ist. Und wo wieder stupide die Umgrenzung der Völker, nicht der Aus-

tausch zwischen ihnen nationales Programm wird, dort klaffen die uralten, halbvergessenen Grenzen der Geschichte als neuaufgerissene Wunden, schneiden sie durch Regionen, über die unzerstörbar der Frieden gebreitet schien, und durch deren Bewohner selbst. Daß viele Völker an ihr siedeln, und zwar nicht bloß eines nach dem anderen und voneinander durch klare Grenzen oder gar durch den Fluß geschieden, ebendas, ihr multinationaler Charakter, machte den Segen der Donau aus, könnte diesen auch fortwirkend bedeuten, und war doch so oft bis in unsere Zeiten herauf nur ihr Fluch.

DER MYTHISCHE STROM

Seit die griechischen Argonauten wagemutig aufbrachen, der Ister, wie die Donau in der Antike hieß, flußaufwärts hinter ihr Geheimnis zu kommen, ist die Donau ein mythischer Strom. Ihr Mythos erzählt von Ursprung und Traum und davon, daß sie in ihrem Verlauf nicht allein Menschen, Städte und Länder verbindet, sondern zwei Welten: Europa und Asien, Abendland und Morgenland. Hölderlin rühmte die Donau als

"melodischen Fluß", der zuwegebrachte, wonach er selber sich sehnsüchtig verzehrte — aus dem von kleingeistigen Fürsten geknechteten Deutschland ins freie, stolze Hellas zu führen. Wie die zwei Welten, von der Donau verbunden, zusammenfinden, dies mochte sich jede Epoche anders erklären. Für Hölderlin beginnt der Strom in Finsternis und Enge, um ins Helle, zum Licht zu fließen — an der Mündung erst erreicht ihm die Donau die Freiheit, erst wenn sie Deutschland, Österreich, Ungarn, den Balkan hinter sich gelassen hat, erblickt sie ihr Ziel, von dem sie doch die ganze Strecke, vorwärtsdrängend, schon weiß: Hellas, stolzes Maß großer Menschen.

Auch für die abertausenden Schwaben, die unter Kaiserin Maria-Theresia ins ferne Hungarland verschickt wurden, Protestanten, unzuverlässige Leute, Arme, die den Frieden der Provinz stören mochten, war der Fluß ein Versprechen von Freiheit. Irgendwo an der Donau, weit weg von den dicht besiedelten Gebieten Schwabens, Bayerns, Ober- und Niederösterreichs, mochten sich weite Räume auftun, die es zu

kolonisieren, den Sümpfen abzutrotzen, gegen heidnischen Zugriff der Türken zu schützen, in Besitz zu nehmen galt. Und doch schien vielen dieser Wehrbauern und Handwerker die Ferne zwar als Versprechen von Wohlstand und Freiheit zu locken, aber auch als fremde, dunkle Welt zu drohen, die erst finsteren Mächten abgewonnen und mit dem Licht der mitgebrachten, der deutschen Kultur erhellt werden mußte. Ob die Donau der Zivilisation entspringt und mit den ostwärts verschickten Menschen die Barbarei immer weiter zurückdrängt oder gerade umgekehrt aus deutscher Enge ans Licht der vorurteilsfreien Antike, des großen weiten Meeres fließt, ob Glück und Freiheit also flußaufwärts oder flußabwärts liegen, ist an verschiedenen Orten der Donau zu verschiedenen Zeiten stets anders beurteilt worden. Die Scharen, die heute aus der Ukraine, aus Rumänien, Bulgarien gen Westen ziehen, suchen mit ihrer Heimat jedenfalls eine gefährliche, in aussichtsloses Elend niedergedrückte Region zu verlassen und streben aus Hölderlins Traumland, das niedergekommen ist, dem Wohlstand zu, der aus der Finsternis von gestern wächst und wächst.

Die Donau hat schon zur Römerzeit eine Grenze mit mächtigen Festungsanlagen gebildet, wie dem gegen die Markomannen aufgezogenen Lauriacum, am Zufluß der Enns in die Donau gelegen und heute Lorch benannt; für 6000 Mann war es damals gebaut worden, und überall an der Donau finden sich solche Reste von gewaltigem Mauerwerk und feiner Kunst der Römer — von der Castra Abusina beim bayrischen Eining über das grandiose Aquincum, eine ausgedehnte Römerstadt in Ungarn, die mit einer mustergültigen Kanalisation und urkundlich mit einem ausgefuchsten System überrascht, nach dem die Betriebskosten der kommunalen Wasserspülung für die Toiletten der privaten Haushalte berechnet wurden, bis hin zu den Denkmälern, die irgendwo in der Walachei wittern, dem Kaiser Trajan, der gegen die Daker zog, zum ewigen Gedächtnis. Zwischen Wien und Bratislava ragt das "Heidentor", Eingang in das sagenhafte Carnuntum, eine imposante Anlage, in der 30.000 Menschen gelebt haben müssen, militärisches und politisches Zentrum, mit einem großen Heerlager für die XIV. Legion und einem größeren

Amphitheater; der Untergang des prächtigen Carnuntum kam vielleicht schnell, denn die Archäologen fanden Jahrhunderte später, ein barockes Motiv vor der Zeit, halbfertig gebackenes Brot im Ofen.

So dramatisch die Donau mit hochragenden Festungen bestückt ist, so oft sie blutig umkämpfte Grenze war, ist es ihr Ansehen doch gerade geblieben, fließend, verbindend, alle Grenzen zu überwinden. Die Legenden der Donau sind allesamt von diesem humanen Mythos des Lebens gespeist, vielleicht mit einer einzigen Ausnahme, dem im Mittelalter entstandenen, in der Neuzeit ideologisch aufgerüsteten Lied von den todesversessenen Nibelungen. Sie, die den frühgriechischen Argonauten um Jahrhunderte verspätet entgegenzogen, sind in unheilvollen Zeiten stets gegen den Donautraum der vielen Völker aufgeboten worden, für das waffenstarrende Germania, das große Deutschland, das sich den Osten untertan machen oder todestrunken untergehen will. Das Lied von den getreuen Nibelungen, den mutigen Ostlandfahrern, singt einen kollektiven Todesmythos und ist so

dem Donaumythos des Lebens und Fließens denkbar fremd entgegengestellt. Daß die Nationalsozialisten die Donau zum "Nibelungenstrom" machten, an dem auch ein Ort namens Mauthausen lag, markiert den schimpflichsten Verstoß gegen Hölderlins melodischen Fluß, der des Lebens Vielfalt preist. Mit den Nibelungen ist ein mächtiger Gegen-Mythos geschaffen worden, der so recht nicht zur Donau, eher an den Rhein paßt (vom dem die Nibelungen ja kamen) oder an irgendeinen Fluß von geringer Intelligenz, dessen Auftrag es in Sagen und Liedern von jeher gewesen sein mag, zwischen zwei Völkern eine Grenze zu bilden, die für natürlich gilt.

Freilich, der Mythos hat seine Wahrheit, aber er ist diese nicht selbst, sie muß ihm erst abgelesen, abgelauscht werden. Wie steht es heute mit der grenzüberwindenden Donau, dem rollenden Völkerband des Liedes? Jedem der zehn Donaustaaten ist der Fluß auch eine Grenze. Zwischen Bayern und Österreich ist die fließende Grenze 21 Kilometer lang, zwischen Österreich und der Slowakei gerade noch sieben, zwischen der Slowakei

und Ungarn immerhin 153; Kroatien und Serbien stehen sich zu beiden Seiten der Donau auf 138 Kilometern gegenüber, und Rumänien beansprucht die Donau gleich gegen alle seine Nachbarn als Grenze: 231 Kilometer gegen Serbien, 399 gar gegen Bulgarien, gerade noch einen hin zu Moldawien und gegen die Ukraine wieder 52 Kilometer. Gewiß, nicht daß es Staatsgrenzen gibt, ist entscheidend, und nicht, ob diese durch einen Fluß gebildet oder mitten im freien Gelände durch einen Schlagbaum markiert werden. Entscheidend ist allein, wie durchlässig die Grenze ist und für wen sie es ist, ob sie, was diesseits und jenseits von ihr geschieht, voneinander absperrt und trennt oder den Austausch nicht nur von Waren, sondern auch von freien Gedanken gleichermaßen ermöglicht wie die freie Bewegung der Anwohner.

Da der Raum, der einst bloß zwischen Österreich und der Türkei aufgeteilt war, heute staatlich zersplittert ist, gibt es keine christlich-abendländische und keine islamische Donau mehr, keinen Fluß der Habsburger und der Osmanen. Die von Prinz Eugen zu einem gewalti-

gen System von Kavernen, unterirdischen Gängen, Mauern ausgebaute Festung Peterwardein, gegenüber von Novi Sad und als Österreichs zentraler Stützpunkt im Kampf gegen die Türken errichtet, ist aus ihrer militärischen Verwendung ebenso schön zum Kulturdenkmal gealtert wie die vielen Festungsanlagen, die die Türken flußabwärts von Peterwardein errichteten, alle übertrumpfend, ein wenig ins Hinterland verlegt, die surreal in den Götterfelsen von Belogradčik geschlagene Feste Kaleto. Mit dem Ersten Weltkrieg, in dem eigene Donauflotten zum Gefecht aufgeboten und insgesamt 847 Schiffe versenkt wurden, sodaß die Donau zum Grab tausender Matrosen wurde, ist auch jener epochale Gegensatz zweier Großstaaten zusammengebrochen. Und doch, die heutigen Konflikte im Donauraum lodern nicht selten just dort auf, wo einst die militärisch erzwungene oder diplomatisch ausgehandelte Grenze zweier Reiche durch Regionen, Dörfer, Familien schnitt. Diese alten Grenzen wurden 1918 aufgehoben, hatten sich aber schon so unheilvoll dem Land eingekerbt, daß sie als innere Bruchlinien durch die neuen Staaten zogen. Bald nach 1945 fiel mit dem Eisernen Vorhang schier unüberwindlich eine zusätzliche Grenze herab, die die Donauländer ein weiteres Mal und entlang einer historisch gänzlich beliebigen Linie trennte. Der abgeblockte Südosten, in sich zerklüftet von den Grenzen, die wechselnde auswärtige Herren über Jahrhunderte immer neu gezogen hatten, geschichtliche Narben, die quer durch Länder und Regionen verliefen und sich bei akuter Reizung unvermittelt neu entzünden konnten, war nun abgesperrt und auf sich selbst zurückgeworfen. Kaum daß der Vorhang von den revoltierenden Menschen des Ostblocks nach über vierzig Jahren gehoben wurde, ist er von deren wohlhabenden Nachbarn im Westen schon wieder niedergelassen worden. Es gibt kein habsburgisches und kein osmanisches Donaureich mehr, keinen Konflikt eines freien und eines unterdrückten Kontinents, keine Koexistenz von parlamentarischen und volksdemokratischen Republiken, kapitalistischen und kommunistischen Staaten; aber es gibt zwei Europa, die von der Donau verbunden werden und neuerlich getrennt sind: ein Europa des Wohlstands schottet sich ab gegen ein Europa der Armut, in dem die Völker aufeinander

schlagen mögen und ein jeder, der es schafft sich loszureißen und die gesperrten Grenzen illegal zu überwinden, sein Glück donauaufwärts zu finden trachtet.

DER IDEOLOGISCHE FLUSS

Zwei Ideologien, die einander bekämpfen, doch zusammengehören, haben seit je darum gerungen, den Donauraum zu beherrschen. Béla Bartók, von der Donau vertrieben, hat sie 1942 in seinem fernen Exil erkannt und beschrieben. Beide schränkten sie ihm die schöpferischen Kräfte des einzelnen wie der Gesellschaft ein, beide hemmten sie just dort, wo sie freie Entfaltung verhießen. Sowohl das "Scheinhafte einer übertreibenden Zusammengehörigkeits-Ideologie" lehnte Bartók ab, als auch deren Gegenstück, "den substantiellen Schein der Nationalcharaktere". Das eine und das andere ist Schein, also Täuschung, die freilich über die Menschen, die ihr erliegen, verheerend in die Wirklichkeit einzugreifen vermag. Eine manchmal fromme Täuschung ist es, die Gebiete der Donau als einheitlichen Kulturraum zu sehen, der nur

der glücklichen politischen Vereinigung harrt; eine fast niemals fromme Täuschung ist es hingegen, wenn jede der kleinen Völkerschaften als autonome Einheit gesetzt wird, in der ein mythischer Nationalcharakter west. Die eine Ideologie vereinnahmt mit menschenfreundlicher Geste, die andere schließt mit grimmiger Miene aus. Die eine sucht unruhig den großen Zusammenschluß eines Imperiums und sich beständig erweiternden Wirtschaftsblocks, die andere ist eitel zufrieden mit der Selbstbezogenheit der Kleinstaaterei. Die übertreibende Zusammengehörigkeit, die Bartók als geistloses Prinzip zuwider war, geht von einer Totalität aus, in der die fruchtbaren Widersprüche abgeschliffen werden; der Kult des mythischen Nationalcharakters wiederum, vor dem es Bartók graute, führt zum Totalitarismus, der Widerspruch gar nicht duldet. Das eine Programm mutet gerade heute sympathisch an, setzt es doch gegen den barbarischen Zerfall auf die vereinigende Synthese. Aber es hat kulturgeschichtlich nicht nur den Berufsstand des schöngeistigen Festredners und europäischen Phrasendreschers ungebührlich bevorzugt, sondern leider auch das andere,

gänzlich unveredelte Programm als sein notwendiges Gegenstück hervorgebracht: die Ranküne der nationalen Borniertheit und Kleinstaaterei. In sie flüchten sich die Opfer des großzügig über alle Unterschiede hinausblickenden Universalismus. Der Ideologie des einheitlichen Donauraumes haben in den letzten zweihundert Jahren viele achtbare, von den schönsten Idealen beflügelte Geister ihren Tribut entrichtet. Der Rumäne Aurel Popovici, enthusiasmiert von der Vorstellung, die Donau selber würde ihre Völker auf einen dauerhaften Frieden verpflichten, veröffentlichte 1906 sein Buch "Die Vereinigten Staaten von Groß-Österreich", in der er die Vision einer Donaukonföderation bis ins bevölkerungsstatistische Detail ausbreitete und sich an den Entwurf einer geopolitischen Ordnung des ganzen Raumes wagte. Noch im Zweiten Weltkrieg geistert die Vorstellung eines großen, föderativ oder gar nach dem Vorbild des Commonwealth aufgebauten Donaureiches durch manche Konferenz von Machtpolitikern und manches Treffen heimwehkranker Emigranten aus den Donaustaaten — und sieht man, welche Ordnung stattdessen über Europa verhängt

wurde, braucht man über ihren Donautraum auch gar nicht weiter zu spotten.

DEUTSCHLAND. REGENSBURG. 1995.
GERMANY. REGENSBURG. 1995.

Und doch hatte Béla Bartók recht, wenn er im politischen Universalismus, über den Donauraum gestülpt, keine Idee sah, die ins Offene führt, sondern eine Ideologie, die sich gegen das Lebendige wendet. Denn die Donau bietet in Wahrheit gerade keinen einheitlichen, sondern einen wunderlich uneinheitlichen Kulturraum, der durch eine frappante Gleichzeitigkeit des Gegensätzlichen geprägt ist. Nachindustrielle und vorindustrielle Regionen und Lebensformen wechseln einander ab, städtische Metropolen und bedrohte ländliche Idyllen, postmoderne und vormoderne Strukturen, unerhörter Reichtum und bitterste Armut, digitalisierte Zonen und solche, die noch nicht einmal elektrifiziert sind; während zwischen Ulm und Budapest Geschäfte bald schon nur mehr per Computer und bargeldlos abgewickelt werden, haben sich in Bulgarien, eine andere Form bargeldlosen Verkehrs, in manchen Belangen das Bic-Feuerzeug und das Päckchen geschmuggelter Marlboro-Zigaretten als Währungsmittel durchgesetzt. Da ist nichts von einheitlichen Lebensverhältnissen, verbindenden Idealen, wenig vom großen gemeinsamen Traum zu erkennen; was die Lebenskultur betrifft und wie sie die tägliche Existenz von Abermillionen Menschen durchformt, hat die Donau zwischen Donaueschingen und Sulina nahezu alles zu bieten, was zwischen Erster und Dritter Welt Menschen heute erpro-

ben möchten oder aber erdulden müssen. Ein Donaureich, in der die Computeringenieurin aus Passau gleichermaßen ihre Heimat sehen könnte wie ein Brackwasserfischer des Donaudeltas, kann es so leicht, wie es ausgedacht wird, nicht geben, und es würde überdies als Herrschaft der finanzstarken Metropolen und industriell fortgeschrittenen Regionen über die Ränder heranrauschen: ein von hochtechnologischer Industrie gesäumter Oberlauf würde in einen Unterlauf übergehen, der durch die künstliche Idylle eines gigantischen Fremdenverkehrsparks führte. Im Westen die Geschäfte, im Osten die Erholung, und indes die hochgestreßten Menschen des Oberlaufs Urlaub im Augebiet des wildromantischen Unterlaufs machen und sich dort von den professionell naturwüchsigen Einheimischen folkloristisch umsorgen lassen, wandern die jungen Anwohner des Unterlaufs dem Westen zu, um sich in der Fremde als Arbeitskräfte zu verdingen. Der politische Universalismus eines geeinten Donaureiches müßte solcherart rasant zerstören, was er gerade zu schützen verspricht: nämlich das Nebeneinander des Verschiedenartigen, die schillernde Fülle an Gegensätzen. Was heu-

te noch ganze Regionen prägt, hätte seinen Platz dann in besonderen Reservaten: Naturmuseum für zivilisationsflüchtige Naturzerstörer.

DER FLUSS DER GLEICHZEITIGKEIT

Die Gleichzeitigkeit des Gegensätzlichen, die den Donauraum prägt, kann fruchtbar und kann furchtbar sein. Allzu oft werden wir heute nur mit dem Furchtbaren konfrontiert, das aus dieser Gleichzeitigkeit springt: mit dem Gegensatz von Luxus hier und Elend dort, oder, überbordend abstrus, von aberwitziger Pracht und ungeheizten Winterwohnungen in ein- und derselben Stadt, etwa im Bukarest des Conducators Ceaucescu, in ein und demselben Staat, etwa der Ukraine von heute, wo einer Handvoll Millionären Millionen Hungerleider gegenüberstehen. Am akuten Gegensatz von weltoffenen wohlhabenden Städten und ihrem von alten Traditionen geprägten Umland haben sich immer wieder Bürgerkriege entzündet, ausbrechend voll jähem Haß, unerwartet, unbegreiflich, selbstzerstörend. Bogdan Bogdanović, einer der bekanntesten Archi-

tekten des Balkans und letzter demokratischer Bürgermeister der Donaustadt Belgrad, hat in den verschiedenen Kriegen, mit denen Jugoslawien so blutig zerfallen ist, auch einen Krieg des Landes gegen die Städte erkannt. Nicht zufällig waren es gerade die toleranten, offenen, architektonisch bedeutenden Städte, die als erste zum Objekt systematischer Zerstörung wurden, Städte, in denen das zeitgenössische urbane Leben sich aus einer langen städtischen Tradition entfalten konnte. Die Provinz, unter das Kuratel strenger, doch vermeintlich gesunder Werte gestellt, rächt sich an der Stadt, in der das Leben von je her anders organisiert und mit dem Verbotenen, der Sünde privilegiert war. Der Sturmangriff auf die Städte mit ihrer praktizierten Toleranz ist denn zu verschiedenen Zeiten in allen Donauländern versucht worden. In den dreißiger Jahren wendet sich der österreichische Katholizismus aus dem ohnmächtigen Grimm über die gottlose Großstadt ins Politische und rüstet gegen das lasterhafte Wien; im östlichen Nachbarland ist es nicht viel anders, die rassistisch verschnittene Ideologie des reinen Ungartums setzt an, das weltoffene Budapest zu

erobern und die Juden, Kosmopoliten, Liberalen, all die Verräter an der mythischen Substanz des ungarischen Volkswesens, hinwegzufegen. Daß sie unübersichtlich ist, bedroht die Moderne, denn der Haß auf sie, wie er im Granatenhagel auf die kosmopolitischen, lebensfrohen Städte kollabiert, ist aus der Furcht vor ihr gewachsen. Der Krieg, dessen Ende heute noch nicht abzusehen ist, endete einst, vor fünfzig Jahren, wie er morgen, übermorgen enden wird: mit einem grausam paradoxen Sieg derer, die ihn gewollt und verloren haben — denn die verhaßten Städte werden auch diesmal in Trümmer liegen, indes das Land, bestimmt vom Jahreszyklus und geordnet nach altem Maß, rasch wieder zum alten Leben erwacht.

Die Gleichzeitigkeit von mächtiger Stadt und traditionellem Umland kann furchtbar freilich auch nach der anderen Richtung schlagen. Die sogenannte "Dorfsystematisierung", mit der Ceaucescu in Wahrheit systematisch die widerständigen Traditionen des Landes brechen, die siebenbürgische Identität zerschlagen wollte, war ein solcher Angriff des

Zentrums auf die Ränder. Ceaucescu war aber nicht nur die
abstoßende Karikatur eines
Vaters der Nation, der seine
Wurzeln im untergegangenen
Dakien wähnte, nicht nur jener
Verfechter einer asiatischen
Despotie, als der er oft charak-
terisiert wurde, sondern er war
auch ein wütend ungelehriger
Schüler des Westens, der diesen stets zu übertrumpfen
suchte. Bukarest hat immer
nach Westen geblickt, über die
Donau hinaus, nach Paris.
Indes in den Vororten von
Bukarest noch die Schafe wei-
deten, haben Bukarester Künstler schon in den zwanziger Jahren aus Eigenem entdeckt, was
in Paris erst später große Mode
werden sollte. Gerade in einem
Land, in dem die Jahrhunderte
aufeinandertrafen und im
Schatten der ersten Wolkenkrat-
zer noch die Selbstversorgung
der Kleingärtnerei blühte, wurde ein so markant modernes
Phänomen wie der Surrealis-
mus entdeckt — nicht als intel-
lektuelles Spiel, sondern als
Möglichkeit, die Wirklichkeit,
wie sie sich aus uralt Überstän-
digem und gänzlich Neuem
zugleich zusammensetzt, zu
deuten und zu verstehen. Die
Bukarester Intellektuellen blickten immer die Donau hinauf
und über deren Quelle hinaus,

sie selbst aber werden von
Europa erst bemerkt, wenn sie
ihre Heimat verlassen und, wie
Eugène Ionescu, Tristan Tzara
oder Emile Cioran, geistig nicht
mehr mit ihren rumänischen
Wurzeln, sondern mit Paris
oder Zürich verbunden werden.
Auch Ceaucescu hat in den
Westen geblickt und diesen mit
der Barbarei der Dorfsystematisierung gleich wieder aufs
lächerlichste zu übertreffen versucht. Es ist bemerkenswert,
daß unter den unzähligen Ver-
stößen gegen Menschenrecht
und Vernunft, die er metho-
disch exekutierte, ausgerechnet
das Wahnziel der rücksichtslo-
sen agrarindustriellen Moderni-
sierung Ceaucescu so wütende
Kritik des Westens eingetragen
hat. Dabei hatte er hier unter
den rumänischen Bedingungen
von Armut und Despotie nur
etwas nachzuholen — und
natürlich gleich wieder kata-
strophal zu überbieten — versucht, was in den wirtschaftlich
entwickelten Ländern des
Westens unter ihren Verhältnissen von Wohlstand und Demo-
kratie längst vollzogen worden
war: die Zerstörung der traditio-
nellen ländlichen Strukturen
mitsamt ihrer alten Architektur
und der störenden Treue der
Menschen zu ihrem Boden, zu
ihrer Arbeit. Was Bauern nie

waren, fungible Arbeitskräfte,
von hier nach dort verpflanz-
bar, sind sie in den Industrie-
ländern längst geworden und
sollten sie nach dem Wunsch
des Conducators auch in Rumänien werden. Wo bei uns der
abstoßende alpenländische
Protzbau stampfend über die
Besonderheiten einer regiona-
len Architektur gezogen ist,
wäre in Rumänien der über
Jahrhunderte gewachsene
Reichtum des feinziselierten
siebenbürgischen Holzbaus
freilich nur durch industriell
verfertigte Elendsware ersetzt
worden . . .

Von Ceaucescus Kampf
gegen die besondere Welt der
Dörfer weiß jedermann, von
den rumänischen Avantgardi-
sten kaum irgendwer. Denn die
Gleichzeitigkeit des Gegensätzlichen wird uns meist nur
bewußt, wenn sie furchtbar,
kaum aber, wenn sie fruchtbar
wirkt. Dabei ist sie die längste
Zeit über für den einzelnen wie
für die Gesellschaft kein zerstö-
rerisches, sondern ein befreien-
des Moment. Was die Donau
mit ihren Ländern und Menschen so anziehend macht, ist
eben die Gleichzeitigkeit, der
sich auf engem Raum entfalten-
de Widerspruch: nicht unbe-

rührte Natur, nicht einheitlich
durchformte Kultur, bietet die
Donau immer das Zugleich, von
Völkern, Religionen, Sprachen,
von Entwicklungsstufen der
Ökonomie, von Traditionen, die

DEUTSCHLAND. NEUBURG. 1959.
GERMANY. NEUBURG. 1959.

nicht preisgegeben, und Auf-
brüchen, die gewagt werden,
von Besonderheiten einer
Volksgruppe, die trotzig
bewahrt, und Verflechtungen
mit der Welt, die als das Selbst-
verständliche gesucht werden.
Wann immer in der Geschichte
die Gleichzeitigkeit aufgehoben
werden sollte — ob von den
Strategen der Macht, die ihre
großen und kleineren Reiche
zur Einheit zwingen wollten;
von den Propheten des Fortschritts, denen der Fluß selber
verdächtig ist, weil er so un-

praktisch windungsreich fließt,
anstatt schnurgerade ins näch-
ste Laufkraftwerk zu strömen;
von den Fanatikern der Ideologie, die sich daran abarbeiten,
daß die Menschen eines Tages

alle im selben Takte denken —,
wann immer die verstörende
Gleichzeitigkeit im Donauraum
aufgehoben werden sollte, war
halb Europa nahe daran, aus
der Balance zu kippen. Die
Donau verträgt keine Hegemo-
nie, auch nicht den hegemonia-
len Anspruch des Gutgemein-
ten. Die Gleichzeitigkeit ist ihr
historisches Schicksal und ihre
Lehre. Dieser Lehre gerecht zu
werden, ist das Einfache, das
oft so schwer fällt.

THE TEACHINGS OF THE DANUBE

Karl-Markus Gauss

THE EXPERIMENTAL RIVER

During the 18th Century a Belgian engineer by the name of Maire had a bold vision. He looked at Europe and the way it was dominated by geographical coincidences: by immovable mountain ranges, by wastefully empty plains, by mighty, yet scarcely exploited rivers; and decided that this was not a good thing. The cool-headed visionary dreamed of a different Europe, and set out for Vienna to win over the Emperor with his dream. And indeed, Josef II, the Habsburgs' freest spirit and most courageous reformer ever to sit in the throne of power, saw, as did his engineer, that there was much room for improvement. To work out in detail how Vienna could become the centre of a network of waterways connecting up the whole of Europe was now Maire's assignment, and he set about draughting plans, calculating and dreaming, and continued to report on the imper-

fections of Mother Nature. The Danube, the European river, was to become the mainstream of Europe, which all other rivers of significance were to be linked up to by means of multiple canals so that the oceans splashing about the edges of the continent could be reached from all directions by water. The plan was to join the Danube with the Adige and the Adriatic in the south, with the Main and Rhine in the West and the Czech river Vltava (or Moldau), the Polish Vistula and the Dniestr in the far land of the Tsars, via a fine network of canals, cuttings, and artificial waterways. At the time, nothing much came of Maire's fervently drawn-up plans, and even to this day there are still some who like to reproach the Belgian engineer for the fact that the Alps still persist in standing in the way between Austria and the Mediterranean, and have never yet been perforated by a canal. Yet even their failed attempt is a sign that the Emperor and his land-reformer

intended to build a Europe that stood under the auspices of the Danube. From thence we are at least left with the knowledge that the Danube knows everything that Europe knows. Nothing new eventuates unless it has been put to the test by the Danube, and nothing old can disappear nor re-emerge from blithe oblivion that has not already sunk into the Danube or mysteriously reappeared on one of its banks. Countless nationalities have settled on the banks of this mighty river, which has seen and suffered everything that the peoples of Central and Southern Europe have achieved or done to themselves or each other. Those things that today make us shudder, the grimace of chauvinism, the hatred of peoples mutually dependent but periodically set against each other, the fanaticism of narrowness, the destruction of nature, the levelling tread of progress; all this we find on the Danube, with a vengeance worse than elsewhere. Yet together with this

RUMÄNIEN. BUKAREST. 1958.
RUMANIA. BUCHAREST. 1958.

horror we also find something about the Danube that fascinates us the world over the beauty of an at times charming, at times harsh, often surprising landscape; its wealth of culture, the multiplicity of its lifestyles, which never cease to influence and enrich but do not override each other; here we find art that has retained its frivolity and a passionate love of life; and oft-proven courageousness, its stubborn strength of developing special qualities in the face of attempts to generalise.

he Danube has known the worst kinds of despots, but has also looked on as they fled head over heels with their lackeys. Much blood has been spilled on the Danube's banks, spilled for property, power and ideology; yet tolerance, too, has over and over again proved effective on the Danube, not only in terms of the intellectual Utopia of enlightened minds or in terms of the political agendas of well-meaning state philosophers, but as a principle of everyday life, as the very wisdom of life practised by so-called ordinary people.

t is a gruesome and puzzling phenomenon that the Danube has not only attracted romantics and naturalists, adventurers, philanderers and lovers, traders and fisherfolk; but also murderers, who have sought out the banks of the Danube to commit their crimes. In every war waged in one of the Danubian countries, people have been dragged out from the country's interior to the Danube for the sole purpose of leading them to a dreadful fate. In January 1942, in the Vojvodinan capital, where since time immemorial various nationalities had lived side by side and peacefully together, the infamous Novi Sad raid was carried out. The city's Jews, along with hundreds of Serbs, were led in a long, eternally still-standing march of misery to the frozen river, where they were then shot dead by units of the Hungarian occupying forces and shoved into the Danube through sawn-out holes in the ice. Similar massacres were to follow in Baja and in Budapest, where for the most horrific and by no means spontaneous, but

extensively planned crimes of violence, the banks of the Danube were chosen every time as the stage for the spectacle, almost as if, by doing so, the crime could be washed out of people's memories. The Vojvodina region, that fertile plain between the Danube, the Tisza and the Sava, was a European experimental lab in which the cohabitation of a great many nations and religions was tried and tested to an exemplary degree, in order to make use of a strip of land and its multi-lingual inhabitants. The outrageous crime against the Jewish and Serbian populations put a bloodthirsty end to an experiment whose final act was sealed by the exilation of the German-speaking population, although they had been living there for 200 years and were quite unjustly made to pay for those crimes that had been committed in the name of the German Reich. Though once a propsperous country, the granary to countless peoples and the silo of contradictory cultural experiences, the Vojvodina has, since the Second World War, not only become poorer through the loss of its Jews, who were driven to destruction, or then through its Swabian population who were

forced to flee the country, but is also economically impoverished. Compared to other regions of the People's Federative Republic of Yugoslavia it was, of course, still wealthy, for Tito had given the Vojvodina the privileged status of an autonomous republic within the Republic of Serbia in an attempt to protect what remained of the old multi-nationality; it was not until his follower removed this status and "discovered" the Vojvodina to be the threatened nucleus of true Serbianism and proceded to abuse it as the military training grounds of Pan-Serbian chauvinism, that it really went to the dogs. What in earlier times seemed to happen of its own accord is today incapable of being rekindled, whether by dictatorial economy or the appeal to nationalism. A region that offered a multiplicity of opportunities for self-fulfillment to Serbs, Hungarians, Jews, Swabians as well as to the in terms of their numbers not insignificant groups of Croats, Romanians, Ukrainians, Slovaks, Bulgarians and even Romany (though these were never treated with equal status), had finally been declared an ethnically cleansed zone. Yet this land fights back, it refusees to accept this new

ideology so inappropriate to its needs and, inevitably, crumbles. Reports are surmounting that claim knowledge about the true origins of life in this region is increasing and that many resist under the surface, despite being daily subjected to the imposition of a brutal and alien homo-genisation process. And just as is the case with the Vojvodina, which had always faced the threat of collapsing into the stupor of barbarism, yet time and again managed to produce people from its midst who carried the whole, undivided wealth of this region inside them; as with the Vojvodina, so too it is with Slovakia, whose capital has three names: Bratislava, Pressburg, Pozsony, and even more nationalities; and thus it is all along the river of Europe: the Danube is in itself an experiment that affects the whole world, what goes awry here can fail anywhere and everywhere; that which succeeds here gives us hope for other places.

THE
STATISTICAL RIVER

Even the historians of antiquity; Ptolemy, Strabo, and Pliny sought to collect and to

review what in their time was known about the Danube. Today, research relating to the Danube has branched out into innumerable disciplines, and thus the amount of available knowledge about a river, a river that is examined, measured and recorded from every imaginable aspect, grows faster than we can keep up with it. Those interested in "Celtic Hill-top Settlements on the Central Danube" will, in any good library, be as quick to find what they are looking for as will those concerned with "History and Technology of Ferries and Bridges over the Austrian Danube"; the ecological sciences deliver yearly warnings with reports on "Wet Bull-dozing in Conservation Areas" or "Strategies for Conservation of a Danubian Fish Fauna". Writings all that are just as deserving of attention as are the multiferious editions of cycling tour guidebooks, that are updated from season to season and now number into the dozens. Apart from specialised research, as recently exhaustively presented in the sizable catalogues for the Upper Austrian Provincial Exhibition in 1994, "Facets of a European River", there is also a steady growth in the flood-banks upon which facile journalism on the subject of the Danube is piled up, and in the face of such educated waffle, the concern as to whether the Danube exists, or whether it is just an invention, becomes undeniably apparent.

irst of all then, a brief retelling of those things that lie buried in legend and myth, but which have doubtless taken place. As always, things started out simply: "With the retreat of the perialpine ocean, the paratethys, at the time of the Lower Freshwater Molasse (sediment) at the turn of the Oligocene into the Miocene from the Swiss and West-Bavarian Molasse-Land, the history of the Danube has its beginnings." The scientist Bernhard Gruber, author of this beautiful piece of Danubian prose, places the beginnings of the present-day Danube, as opposed to the "Pre-Danube", that gigantic, slowly eastward-flowing complex of rivers, lakes and pools, at approximately eleven million years before our time. These eleven million years had to almost entirely go by before the first human reached the Danube. This person, who suddenly emerged during the last Ice Age from the darkness of prehistory, in

the period referred to by scholars as Würm (or Uppermost Pleistocene) and casually estimated as the roughly one hundred thousand years between 120 000 and 12 000 BC, should by no means be thought of as either a genuine Austrian, a full-blooded Serb or whatever other kind of purified nationalist of prehistoric times. Into the dark from which they came were whole hordes of peoples doomed to disappear, after having made their way through to the Danube and settling on its banks for a few years or a few centuries, leaving behind them splendiferous works of goldsmith craft, burial sites or nothing but their magical names: Pechenegs, Cumans, Sazygens, Khazars, the artistic Avars, the mighty Dacians . . .

lthough its two sources, the Brege and the Brigach in the Black Forest as well as its third source in Donaueschingen have eternally been at the centre of localised patriotic conflict, and cannot really be determined with any degree of precision, strangely nevertheless, geographers today know precisely that the Danube covers a stretch of 2888 kilometres, making it the second longest

river in Europe after the Volga. Its absolute slope of 678 metres enables it to flow usually gently, but again along some stretches, wildly; a programme that is but mediocrely described by the statistical mean slope of 123.53 centimetres / kilometre. Whereas in Ulm, where its width of approximately forty metres still makes it little more than a provincial German river, by the time it reaches Turnu Severin on the Romanian-Serb border it has expanded to a mighty force of 1300 metres in width. And though it passes through Vienna at a comparatively high speed of eight kilometres an hour, by the time it has reached the Danube Delta with its countless sidestreams and the ebb and flow of the river into the sea, it has almost come to a standstill. Even in antiquity Pliny made famous the wealth of fish-fauna the Danube had to offer, and sang the praises of the beluga, a fish of up to nine metres in length, as did Albertus Magnus during the Middle Ages in his compendium "De Animalibus"; the fact that Vienna's Fish Market was once able to offer fifty different kinds of fish for sale can be read in the chronicles of astonished travellers of the early modern period; meanwhile, in

the 20th century, the long-respected profession of the Danubian fisherman has, in many places, died out, particularly in the wealthier upper course of the Danube; which is why, for those countless anglers who persist in congregating along its banks, it has become necessary to introduce the term "sport fisherman". The Danube's history of ship transport dates back to ancient times, when originally the main goods to be transported were those basic materials to be found near the river, as well as wood, wine, ore and the like. Barge transport led to the flourishing of settlements along the river and also to the noble art of shipbuilding, a craft that brought prosperity not only to individual families of craftsmen, but to whole villages and towns. Around the year 1800, however, in the Austrian town of Persenberg, four new ships emerged from an early industrial shipmaker's yard every month. And almost as old as ship travel and shipbuilding are the attempts to master the two dangers threatening the regular exchange of goods along the Danube: attempts were made to overcome the river's dangerous pitfalls by means of small and large-scale regulating measures, while at

the same time conventions were devised with the intention of getting around the alternating currents of political situations and guaranteeing the smooth flow of navigational traffic according to reliable and immutable rules. Right up to the 19th century, navigators stood in fear of rapids, whirlpools and sudden narrowings in the river's course, such as those near Grein in the Austrian region of Strudengau, whose very name - reminiscent of vortices - is implicit of the horror felt by the boatspeople, or before the unique and imposing natural backdrop of the Iron Gate where the Balkans and the Carpathians crash into each other; on the other hand, certain rules usually remained intact, despite many a conflict and the embittered animosity between states and political systems, even in the midst of the Cold War, as laid down in a convention relating to/ on ship transport on the Danube in order to secure general usage of the waterway and the river's international status. During the forty years between 1950 and 1990, the tonnage of manufactured goods, raw materials and freight transported on the Danube has nevertheless increased eightfold. And thanks to the Rhine-Main-Danube-Canal and its connections, the networking of Europe via canals which the Austrian engineer and his emperor dreamed of in the 18th century, has at least northwardly become reality. As a consequence of the construction of hydroelectric power plants, in Bavaria alone, there were at the last count twenty that had been built, and the excessive industrial exploitation of the river, the Danube has in the past decades become ecologically severely damaged and the diversity of species has been drastically reduced. On the other hand, the thus endangered river has, in all its thoroughfare countries, been rediscovered by people who have only come to realise through the tangible threat of its loss what it means and has always meant for the life of their region, and that there is no guarantee of continued prosperity for them if poisons and sewerage continue to be thoughtlessly tipped into the river. Admittedly, the Danube still has riverside wetlands, untouched and extensive, the likes of which will scarcely be found elsewhere on this densely populated part of the planet. To be sure, even Theodor W. Adorno gave himself over to

murmured incantations, noticeably enthralled as he was by his experience of nature when, in the excited year 1967, he was taken to the Danube's riverside meadows near Vienna: "How puzzling is the great loneliness on the river, though but a few kilometres from Vienna. Eastwards as we are here, a Puszta-like spell keeps people away from landscape and flora as if the endlessly open space did not want to be disturbed."

THE SUPRANATIONAL RIVER

Had that previously mentioned engineer Maire embarked upon an adventurous journey from the source of the Danube to its mouth, he would have passed through numerous countries, heard scores of languages, could have prayed according to many different rites, but on his ways along the river he would have had but one border to pass: the upper course of the Danube belonged to the Emperor, the lower course was reigned over by the Sultan. Still today, many things continue to serve as a reminder of their centuries-long struggle even in the most secluded villages of the backwoods and

of course in the cities along the river. Thus, in many places, that old animosity symbolised on the portals of the parish church of St Stephen in Tulln on the Danube, where an Austrian double-headed eagle has for centuries held a Turk's skulls in its claws, has never been laid to rest. Since then, when Austria blossomed into the Danube Monarchy and the Ottoman Empire was not yet prepared to relinquish its European bastions, the number of states the Danube flows through has increased considerably. These were ten at the last count, a feat unmatched by any other river on this earth.. Though they may, such as the Yangtzekiang, the Nile, the Misssissippi or the Amazon, be more than double the length of the Danube, but ten states? If we take, in addition to Germany, Austria, Hungary, Romania and Bulgaria, also the recently evolved Slovakia, the republics resulting from the disintegration of Yugoslavia, the republics of Croatia and Serbia, and if we add those countries formed out of the bankrupt mess of the Soviet Union, Ukraine, and Moldavia, we arrive at ten. Yet these could easily become fifteen without the slightest warning, and even

at twenty Danubian states, the new lords of the ever-diminishing, ever more patriotic states will not have arrived at that (one) goal they are all dreaming of, of an ethnically unified, racially purified state formation, in each of which one single national state would be endowed with unheard of blissfulness, having only one blessed holy language, only one sanctified religion, one populist despot and one single exemplary state of stupidity to be able to live completely alone among one's own kind.

he countryside along the Danube itself, having been formed as much by history as by nature, contradicts the compulsory idea of a continent that is made up of many different national states. For over the centuries these peoples, nationalities and religious communities have been moving on and along the Danube. On ships, whose human freight was often dragged into the river's depths, on horse-drawn carts that drove through disease-stricken regions, trudging on foot as legionaries and mercenaries; fleeing from religious persecution, driven by the yearning for a land of their own, sent or

lured into foreign lands by those in power; people have always been on the move in the Danube countries. And if they settled down happily somewhere and founded a community, there were people already living in the next village who were not their equal in language nor in ritual but were so in their destiny. Bound here from somewhere or other, full of hope that they might have found their place on this earth where they could stay, work, multiply, procreate, reproduce and earn their own prosperity for their own kin on fertile ground. The nationalities in the Danube area are completely inseparably interwoven with each other and the question of where someone comes from, what language his grandparents spoke or in what place of worship his parents said their prayers can usually no longer be answered by any kind of genealogy. Everywhere on the Danube there are to be found German-speaking Swabians who answer to the Hungarian name Toth or the Slovakian Prajko, whereas their Croatian neighbours carry the German name Majster, the Hungarians have the good Serbian name of Vidovic, and the Romanians occasionally carry Slovak names; and the Jews, once the binding nationality between the peoples along this people-linking river, who bore names in a multitude of languages and were yet able to preserve them, and of course there is not only what is to be expected, namely, Catholic Croatians and Orthodox Serbs, but also Scocatians and Bunjevatians who felt themselves to be Serbs but are of Catholic denomination, and Pomaks who, though they are Bulgarians, are not adherents to the Bulgarian Orthodox rite, but are Islamified and therefore sometimes privileged and sometimes disregarded Bulgarians, and pious Lipovans who came to the Black Sea from the interior from the Russian steppes and the dust of Galicia for the sake of their strict religious faith, and in whose hands almost the entire fishing industry of the delta is to be found today. As well as countless other peoples who in terms of language, religion and customs do not merely belong to just one or the other but to two or three nationalities at the same time and woe betide us if those times unexpectedly return in which each individual is forced to decide on just one of these, when his very identity will intrinsically be torn apart by such

a decision. The national identity is in many cases, at least in the Balkans, an uncertain matter, and perhaps it is precisely for this reason that it is sometimes so vehemently emphasised, because in the Danube area it has something of a flowing quality without any reliable limitation. The hatred of one's neighbour, as is again being politically cultivated and mobilised, is also a form of self-hatred directed at the insecurity, the uncertainty and the flowing, see-sawing quality of one's own existence. Even so, the ethnic cleansings of both the present and the future can in no way be conducted with such barbarism that the Danube area should evolve into national states unable to contain within their borders the many different ethnicities, so-called minorities, who have lived there since the dawn of history. Whenever the mania for ethnic purity rears up, baring its teeth, it rams just as quickly into those people in whom the multi-ethnic inheritance has been mixed to the greatest advantage. And wherever the reorganisation of borders between peoples instead of the exchange between them is mindlessly made into the national agenda, there the ancient, half-forgotten frontiers

of history gape like re-opened wounds; there too they slice through regions over which peace had seemed to have been spread out like an indestructible layer, and through its very inhabitants. The fact that many peoples have settled along it, and not just one after the other, separated from each other by clear borders or even by the river itself, but this very fact of its multinational character has constituted the blessing of the Danube, and it could continue to have this significance, though often even to this day it has only been its curse.

THE
MYTHICAL RIVER

Ever since the Greek argonauts daringly set out up river to discover the secret of the Ister, as the Danube was known in antiquity, it has been a mythological river. Its myth tells of origins and dreams, and that its course not only links people, towns and countries, but also two worlds, Europe and Asia, occident and orient. Hölderlin praised the Danube as a "melodious river" that managed to achieve that very goal which consumed him with longing, to lead out of a Germany enslaved

by small-minded dukes and their principalities into the free and proud Hellas. Each era has its own explanation for the way in which these two worlds linked by the Danube come together. In Hölderlin's view the river begins in darkness and narrowness and flows on into brightness and light. Only at the river's mouth, he says, does the Danube attain freedom. Only after it has left Germany, Austria, Hungary and the Balkans behind, does it have its goal in sight which it has known, while surging forward, for the whole course: Hellas, the proud nation of great people. But for those too, the countless thousands of Swabians sent by Empress Maria-Theresa to the far-off land of the Magyars; Protestants, unreliable people, poor people, who were able to have it in their power to disturb the peace of the countryside: for all these people the river was a promise of freedom. Somewhere on the Danube, far away from the densely-populated regions of Swabia, Bavaria, Upper and Lower Austria, wide open spaces which needed to be colonised and wrested from the marshlands, which were to be protected from the heathen attacks of the Turks and which were to be taken into posses-

sion. Yet, to many of these peasant-soldiers and craftsmen, the distant land seemed a tempting promise of prosperity and freedom, but also a threateningly strange and dark

RUMÄNIEN. BUKAREST. 1958.
RUMANIA. BUCHAREST. 1958.

world that had been first gained from dubious sinister powers and had to be brightened by the light of the German culture they had brought with them. Whether the Danube originates from civilisation and, together with those people who were sent eastwards, pushes barbarism ever further away, or contrarily, whether it flows out of German narrowness towards the light of unprejudiced antiquity and the great wide open sea; whether happiness and freedom are to be found up stream or downstream has always been seen differently in the various points along the Danube and at various times. The masses of people that today make their way from the Ukraine, Romania and Bulgaria towards the West, seek in leaving their home countries to leave a dangerous region suppressed into hopeless misery, and strive by abandoning Hölderlin's now-demised dreamland, for the prosperity that has grown and continues to grow from the darkness of yesteryear.

lready in Roman times the Danube had formed a frontier with mighty fortifications, such as the Lauriacum which was erected against the Marcomanni, situated at the confluence of the Enns into the Danube and known today as Lorch. At the time it was built for six thousand men and all along the Danube such remains can be found of imposing masonry and the refined art of the Romans, from the Castra Abusina near

the Bavarian town of Eining, to the grandiose Aquincum, an extensive Roman city in Hungary that surprises the visitor with a model canalisation system and also with documents of a cleverly contrived system for calculating the running costs for the communal water supply used in flushing toilets in private households, and goes on down to the monuments that rot away somewhere in the vastness of the Wallachian plain as an eternal reminder of the emperor Trajan, who led his troops against the Dacians. Between Vienna and Bratislava the "Gateway of the Pagans" stands out, the entranceway into the fabulous Carnuntum complex, an imposing camp in which thirty thousand people must have lived, a political and military centre with a large army camp for the XIVth Legion, and a rather large amphitheatre. The splendid Carnuntum may have met with a rapid demise, since centuries later archaeologists found (a baroque motif ahead of its time) half-baked bread still in the ovens.

hile the Danube is dramatically decorated with towering fortresses, having

often been a frontier fought over in bloody battles, it has still retained its image of a flowing and linking transcender of borders. The legends of the Danube have all been informed by this human myth of life, perhaps with one single exception, that song which originated in the Middle Ages and which in modern times has been ideologically refuelled, that of the death-obsessed Nibelungen. These people, who belated by centuries, went to battle against the early Greek argonauts, have in times of trouble always been reinvoked against the Danubian dream of multi-ethnicity, for the saber-rattling Germania, that Greater Germany which wished to make the East subservient to itself, or else perish in a deathly drunken stupor. The song of the Nibelungen, faithful unto the death, those brave, courageous crusaders in eastern lands, sings of a collective death myth, and is thus as far removed as can be imagined from the Danubian myth of life and flowing. The fact that the National Socialists turned the Danube into a "River of the Nibelungen" on whose banks a place called Mauthausen lay, marks the most despicable affront to Hölderlin's melodious

river that praises life in all its variations. The creation of the Nibelungen resulted in a powerful anti-myth that seems hardly appropriate to the Danube but rather to the Rhine (where the Nibelungen actually came from) or to some other river of lesser intelligence whose task in sagas and songs may, from time immemorial, have been to create a border between two peoples that was considered natural.

f course, there is truth in the myth, but the myth is not truth in itself, the truth must be gleaned from it, must be extracted from it. And what is the situation today regarding the Danube as a transcender of borders, the rolling ribbon binding peoples, as in the song? For each of the ten Danubian states the river is also a border, between Bavaria and Austria, the flowing border is twenty-one kilometres long, between Austria and Slovakia it is just on seven. Between Slovakia and Hungary nevertheless, a hundred and fifty-three, Croatia and Serbia oppose each other on both sides of the Danube for a full one hundred and thirty-eight kilometres, and Romania fences itself in with

the Danube as a border against all its neighbours: against Serbia for two-hundred and thirty-one kilometres, for as many as three-hundred and ninety-nine against Bulgaria, just one on the border to Moldavia, and again fifty-two kilometres against Ukraine. To be sure, it is not significant whether there are state borders and whether these are formed by a river or marked by a barrier-arm in the middle of the landscape. The only factor of significance is how permeable the border is and who it is permeable for, whether it separates and locks away that which happens on one side or the other, or whether it makes possible the exchange not only of goods but also of free thoughts in addition to the freedom of movement of those who live alongside it.

ecause the space that was once divided up between Austria and Turkey is today broken up into different states, there is no longer a Catholic-Christian and an Islamic Danube, no river of the Habsburgs and the Ottomans. The fortress of Peterwardein (Petrovaradin), built up by Prince Eugene of Savoy to form a magnificent system of caverns, caves, subterranean corridors and walls, situated opposite Novi Sad and erected as Austria's essential stronghold in the battle against the Turks, has aged from its times of military employ to become a beautiful cultural monument, as have the many fortress-complexes that the Turks built downriver from Peterwardein, the most beautiful of all being Kaleto fortress, set back slightly into the hinterland and surreally hidden within the Rocks of the Gods at Belogradcik. Beginning in the First World War when the Danube's own fleets were sacrificed to the battle and a total of eight-hundred and forty-seven ships were sunk, making the Danube the grave of thousands of sailors, so too, the epoch-making contrast of two major states broke down, and yet the present-day conflicts in the Danube region flare up not infrequently precisely in those places where the martially enforced or diplomatically negotiated border between two nations cut through provinces, villages and families. These old borders were lifted in 1918, but had already etched themselves into the land in such an ominous way that they ran through the new states like internal perforation lines. Soon

after 1945, as the Iron Curtain descended across Europe, a new and seemingly insuperable boundary was formed, which once again divided the Danube countries, this time along historically completely arbitrary lines. The blocked-off Southeast, fissured within itself by the borders drawn and re-drawn by ever-changing foreign rulers over the course of centuries, historical scars that ran across countries and regions, threatening to become freshly inflamed if acutely provoked, was now encapsulated and thrown back upon itself. Scarcely had the curtain been lifted from the uprising people of the Eastern Block after more than forty years, than it was let down again by their wealthy neighbours in the West. There is no longer a Habsburgian or an Ottoman kingdom on the Danube, there is no conflict of one free and one suppressed continent, no co-existence of parliamentary and people's democratic republics, capitalist and communist states; but there are two Europes, both linked by the Danube and recently separated: a Europe of prosperity and civilisation shuts itself off against a Europe of poverty, in which its different peoples may clash with each other and where

everyone who manages to break loose and transverse the closed borders illegally hopes to find his fortune in the upper courses of the Danube.

THE
IDEOLOGICAL RIVER

Two opposing ideologies that nevertheless go hand in hand have fought since earliest times to dominate the Danube region. Béla Bartók, evicted from his home on the Danube, recognised and described them in 1942 from his distant exile. To him, both ideologies limited the creative strengths of the individual as well as of society, inhibiting each at just the point where they seemed to show the greatest promise. Bartók rejected both the "superficiality of an exaggerating ideology of belonging", but also its opposite, "the substantial appearance of national characteristics". Both the former and the latter are mere appearance, and therefore deception, that is freely capable of gravely interfering in reality through the people who are its victims. It is at times a pious illusion to see the regions of the Danube as a unified cultural area waiting solely for blissful political reunion. On the other

hand, it is almost never a pious illusion when each of the small ethnic groups is made into an autonomous unit in which a mythical national character resides. The one ideology takes in everything with a humane gesture, the other excludes all with a grim countenance. The first frantically seeks the great rejoining of an empire with continually extending economic blocks, the other is vainly satisfied with the egocentricity of small-state particularism.

he exaggerating principle of belonging, which Bartók rejected as mindless, assumes a totality in which useful contradictions are honed down. On the other hand, the cult of the mythical national character, which Bartók had a horror of, leads to totalitarianism that allows no contradictions at all. The first programme may, today in particular, seem appealing, as it emphasises the unifying synthesis as an antidote to barbaric disintegration. Yet from a cultural and historic point of view it has not only given precedence to the professional league of platitudinous speechifiers and European purveyors of hackneyed phrases, but unfortunately also produced

the other, completely unrefined programme as its necessary counterpart: the rancourousness of national tunnel vision and small-statehood. It is into this that the victims of universalism, that so generously overlooks all differences, flee. During the last two hundred years many respectable minds, moved by the most beautiful ideals, have paid their tribute to the ideology of a unified Danube region. The Romanian Aurel Popovici, enthused by the idea that the Danube itself would oblige its people to permanent peace, published his book, "The United States of Greater Austria", in 1906, in which he propagated the vision of a Danubian confederation, going into statistical details of the population and even daring to propose a model of a geopolitical order of the entire region. During the Second World War too, the image of a large federative Danubian kingdom, possibly even modelled on the Commonwealth, was circulated through many a conference of power politicians and many a meeting of homesick emigrants from the Danubian states, and in light of the order that was actually imposed on Europe instead, there is no further cause to mock their Danubian dream.

And yet Béla Bartók was right by seeing in the kind of political universalism to be slapped on the Danubian region not an idea leading into the open but as an ideology directed against the very forces of life. For, truth to tell, the Danube does not exactly offer a heterogeneously united, but rather an amazingly ununited cultural region marked by a striking simultaneity of opposing characteristics. Post-industrial and pre-industrial regions and lifestyles alternate one with the other, city metropolises and endangered country idylls, post-modern and pre-modern structures, untold wealth and abject poverty, digitalised zones and areas that have not even got electricity; whereas between Ulm and Budapest business transactions are soon to be conducted only by plastic money, i.e. cashlessly, in Bulgaria another means of cashless trade has established itself, in some cases the Bic lighter or the packet of smuggled Marlboro cigarettes serving as the currency unit. Here there is not much to be seen of unified living conditions, linking ideals, and little of a great mutual dream. As regards the way of life and how it moulds the day-to-day existence of millions of people, the Danube has

almost everything to offer between Donaueschingen and Sulina which modern-day people between the First and Third Worlds may like to try out or may have to put up with. But it is easier said than done to produce a Danubian kingdom which the computer engineer from Passau can equally call her home as can a fisherman in the swampy backwaters of the Danube delta, and furthermore a dominance of the financially powerful metropolises and industrially advanced regions would cause the pot to boil over at the rims, advancing like a tidal wave: an upper course hemmed by high-tech industry would overflow into a lower course leading through the artificial idyll of a gigantic tourist park. Business in the West, pleasure in the East, and while the highly-stressed people of the upper course take their holidays in the riverside parks of the wildly romantic lower course, folkloristically cared for by the professionally rustic natives, the lower course's young population sets out for the West to seek its fortune as labourers in the foreign lands. The political universalism of a united Danubian kingdom would thus rapidly destroy the very thing it promises to pro-

tect, namely the coexistence of the dissimilar, the sparkling richness of contrast. That which exemplifies complete regions would only find room in special reservations; a nature museum for destroyers of nature hoping to flee civilisation.

THE RIVER OF SIMULTANEITY

The simultaneity of the opposing characteristics that exemplify the Danube area can be both fruitful and frightful. These days, we are all too often confronted with the frightful aspect that emerges from this simultaneity: with the contrast of luxury here and misery there, or to put it more bluntly, of ludicrously exaggerated splendour and unheated appartments in winter in one and the same city, such as in the Conducator Ceaucescu's Bukarest; and in one and the same state, such as modern-day Ukraine, where a handful of billionaires stand in opposition to millions of starving people. The acute contrast between worldly, prosperous cities and the surrounding countryside full of old traditions has always ignited civil wars, breaking out full of spontaneous hatred, unexpected,

incomprehensible and self-destructive. Bogdan Bogdanović, one of the most eminent architects of the Balkans, and the last democratic mayor of the Danubian city of Belgrade, recognised in the various wars that have torn Yugoslavia apart so bloodly, a war of the countryside against the cities. It was by no means coincidence that it was precisely the tolerant, open-minded, architecturally significant cities that became the first objects of the systematic destruction, cities in which contemporary urban life was able to flourish from a long metropolitan tradition, the provinces placed under the cudgel of strict, but supposedly healthy values, venges itself upon the city, where life has always been differently organised and which has always enjoyed the forbidden privilege of a life in sin. The assault on the cities with their practised tolerance has been attempted at various times in all of the Danube countries. In the thirties, Austrian Catholicism turned from its powerless fury at the godless metropolis to politics, and armed itself against vice-ridden Vienna; in its neighbouring country to the east, things were not much different. The racist mixture of ideologies of pure Magyarism

set about to conquer the urbane city of Budapest and to rid it of Jews, cosmopolitans, liberals and all traitors to the mythical substance of the essential Hungarian people. The fact that it is confusing threatens modernism, for the hatred towards it as expressed in the shellfire on the cosmopolitan, colourful city has grown out of the very fear of it. The war, whose end is not yet in sight, ended once, fifty years ago, just as it will end tomorrow and the next day; with a cruelly paradoxical victory of those who wanted the war and lost it, for the much-reviled cities will again this time be reduced to rubble, whereas the country, determined as it is by the cycle of the seasons and arranged and organised according to old standards, will quickly recover its old energy.

he simultaneity of the powerful city and the traditional countryside can of course also strike a fearsome note in the other direction, the so-called policy of "village systematisation", with which Ceaucescu veritably intended to systematically break the resistant traditions of the country, and to destroy the identity of the people of Transsylvania, was such an attack by the central powers on the periphery. Ceaucescu, however, was not just the disgusting caricature of the Father of the Nation, who considered himself a descendant of the ancient (and now extinct) Dacians. He was not only the defender of Asiatic despotism, as he was often described, but he was also a raging, undisciplined apprentice of the West, who was constantly trying to outdo his master. Bukarest had always looked to the West, beyond the Danube, to Paris. While the sheep were still grazing in the suburbs of Bukarest, Bukarestian artists in the twenties had already discovered something that was later to become the height of fashion in Paris. Of all countries it was this, where the centuries collided on top of each other, and in the shadow of the first skyscraper, the self-sufficiency of small-scale gardening was blossoming; where such a startlingly modern phenomenon as surrealism was discovered, not as an intellectual game but as a means of interpreting and understanding reality as it was, composed of ancient overhangs and completely new elements. The Bukarestian intellectuals have always looked upriver of the Danube and beyond its source. They themselves, how-

ever, are only noticed by Europe at all when they have left their home country and, like Eugene Ionescu, Tristan Tzara or Emile Cioran, are mentally no longer associated with their Romanian roots, but with Paris or Zurich. Ceaucescu, too, looked to the West and attempted, by means of the barbarism of his "village systemisation", to once again outdo it in the most ludicrous way. It is remarkable that, considering the countless affronts to human rights and rationality which he methodically executed, this particular insane goal of the ruthless agrarian-industrial modernisation brought Ceaucescu such angry criticism from the West. Though here he had only tried, under the Romanian circumstances of poverty and despotism to make up for, and naturally, of course, to catastrophically exaggerate, the very thing that had long since been completed in the economically-developed countries of the West under their conditions of prosperity and democracy: the destruction of traditional rural structures, together with their old architecture and the annoying loyalty of the people to their soil and their work. Functional labourers, something that farmers had never been, easily transplanted from here to

there, is what they had long since become in the industrialised countries and this is what they were also to become in Romania, according to the wishes of their Conducator. Whereas here in our country, the repulsive Alpine showcase building has stampeded over the unique regional special qualities of architecture, in Romania the richness of their centuries-old finely filigreed Transsylvanian wooden buildings would of course have been replaced by an industrially manufactured, poor quality product.

eaucescu's battle against the peculiar world of the villages is known to one and all, but hardly anyone knows about the Romanian avant-garde. For we usually only become aware of the simultaneity of opposing qualities when they are frightful, but hardly when they are fruitful. And this though for most of the time it is, for the individual as well as for society, a liberating moment rather than a destructive one. What makes the Danube so attractive with all its countries and people is its very simultaneity, its contradictions unfolding within a narrow space: neither mere unsullied nature,

nor just a single uniformly streamlined culture, the Danube always offers a coexistence of all peoples, religions, languages, and different stages of economic growth all at the

RUMÄNIEN. SULINA. 1994.
RUMANIA. SULINA. 1994.

same time, traditions that are not relinquished and new beginnings that are daringly embarked upon, peculiarities of a group of peoples who stubbornly hold on to things and interweavings with the world that are sought without question. Whenever in history attempts are made to remove the simultaneity, whether by power strategists who wish to railroad their large or smaller kingdoms into unity, whether the prophets of progress who find the river itself a problem because it

flows in such an impractical winding course instead of streaming straight as a die into the nearest hydroelectric power station; or by the fanatic followers of the ideology who work

themselves to the bone in the hope that one day people will all think in the same rhythm; whenever this unsettling simultaneity in the Danubian area is to be abolished, half of Europe has always been about to tip off balance. The Danube cannot tolerate any hegemony, and not even the hegemonial claim of those who mean well. Its simultaneity is its historical fate and its teaching. And to do justice to this teaching is one of those simple things that often prove so difficult.

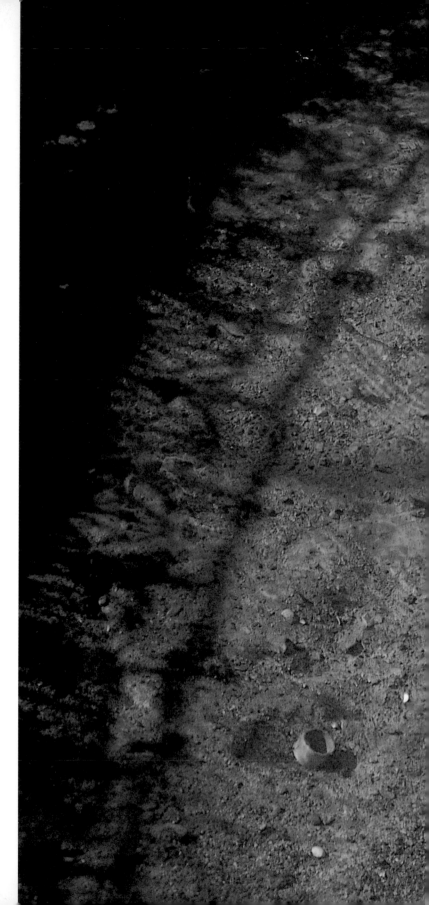

DEUTSCHLAND. DONAUESCHINGEN. 1994.
Die Donauquelle im Fürstenbergschen Park. Das Wasser fließt in die aus Furtwangen kommende Breg. Beide vereinen sich einen Kilometer weiter mit der in St. Georgen im Schwarzwald entspringenden Brigach: hier beginnt unwidersprochen die Donau. Ein Stein am Ufer kündet an: 2.778 Kilometer bis zum Schwarzen Meer.

GERMANY. DONAUESCHINGEN. 1994.
Source of the Danube in the Park of the Princes of Fürstenberg. These waters run into the small river Breg, coming from Furtwangen. Roughly a mile later they are united with the Brigach arriving from St. Georgen im Schwarzwald. From this point on, the river is definitely the Danube. A stone marker on the left bank announces: 2.778 kilometers to the Black Sea.

DEUTSCHLAND. IN DER NÄHE VON DIETHFURT. 1958.
Die junge Donau auf dem Weg durch die Schwäbische Alb.

GERMANY. NEAR DIETHFURT. 1958.
The young Danube making its way through the Swabian Alb.

DEUTSCHLAND. FURTWANGEN. 1995.

Oben: Wiese und Haus von Maria Hoch. Bregquelleneinfassung unter dem Hotel Kolmenhof.

Unten: Herr Dobl an der Theke seines Kolmenhofhotels.

Das Pamphlet der Maria Hoch klärt ihrer Meinung nach den umstrittenen Sachverhalt um die wirkliche Donauquelle. Unter ihrem Haus, in der großen Wiese, die ihr gehört, entspringen mehre Quellen. Jene sind in einer Felsenumrahmung auf dem Grundstück des Nachbarn, Bruder des Besitzers des ein paar Schritte entfernten Kolmenhofhotels, dekorativ eingefaßt und als 'Breg Donauquelle' "zur Besichtigung freigegeben", bevor sie den Weg nach Donaueschingen antreten.

GERMANY. FURTWANGEN. 1995.

Top: Meadow and house belonging to Maria Hoch. Foreground: Rocks frame the source of the Breg under the Hotel Kolmenhof.

Bottom: Maria Hoch's neighbour, Mr. Dobl, at the bar of his Hotel Kolmenhof.

Maria Hoch maintains that her pamphlet clears the disputed question of the source of the Danube. Under her house, in her meadow, bubble a lot of springs whose waters are collected in a rock-framed basin on the property of her neighbour, "free to be viewed" by visitors. From there they make their way to Donaueschingen as the river Breg.

DEUTSCHLAND. DONAUESCHINGEN. 1995.

Fürstenbergische Donauquellen-Souvenirs.

GERMANY. DONAUESCHINGEN. 1995.

Souvenirs. Source of Danube, Park of the Princes of Fürstenberg.

DEUTSCHLAND. FURTWANGEN. 1995.

Links: Maria Hoch mit Donauquellenpamphlet.

"Oft wurde hin- und hergestritten, welche die echte Donauquelle ist, die in Donaueschingen oder die in Furtwangen. Genau genommen haben beide Meinungen recht. Aber die Breg ist der längste Zufluß zur Donau."

GERMANY. FURTWANGEN. 1995.

Left: Maria Hoch holding her pamphlet concerning the question of the source of the Danube.

"Many times people have been disputing which is the real source of the Danube, the one in Furtwangen or the one in Donaueschingen. In a way, both are right. But the Breg is the longest tributary."

DEUTSCHLAND. KELHEIM. 1995.
Oben: Flohmarkt bei der Donaudampferanlegestelle.
Unten: Regensburg. 1995. Süßes mit herben Inschriften. Maidult.

GERMANY. KELHEIM. 1995.
Top: Fleamarket near the pier for Danube steamers.
Bottom: Regensburg. 1995. Stall with gingerbread hearts at annual May fair.

DEUTSCHLAND. SIGMARINGEN. 1959.

Unter der Bismarck-Statue feiern gerade aus dem Wehrdienst entlassene junge Männer die wiedergewonnene zivile Freiheit und nehmen gelassen die Glückwünsche der neu eingezogenen Rekruten entgegen.

GERMANY. SIGMARINGEN. 1959.

Under a statue of Bismarck young men celebrate the end of their compulsory service in the army and accept the congratulations of new recruits.

DEUTSCHLAND. SIGMARINGEN. 1995.

Die erste Burg über dem Donaufelsen entstand im 10. Jahrhundert als Sitz der Herren von Sigmaringen. Im 16. Jhdt. folgten die Grafen von Hohenzollern; 1850 wurde die Burg an die preußische Linie abgetreten. Jetzt Fürstlich-Hohenzollersches Museum.

GERMANY. SIGMARINGEN. 1995.

In the tenth century the first castle was built on the dominating rock above the Danube as seat of the Herrn von Sigmaringen. In the 16th century they were succeeded by the Counts of Hohenzollern; in 1850 the castle was given over to the Prussian branch of the family. Now it is the Museum of the Princes of Hohenzollern.

DEUTSCHLAND. ULM. 1959.

Das Münster ist der Sakralbau mit dem höchsten Turm Europas. Bauzeit 1377-1533. Ein Wasserspeier teilt den Blick auf Stadt und Donau.

Dieser Fleck am Fluß war seit der Jungsteinzeit besiedelt, von Kelten, Alemannen, Franken. 1274 erhielt die Stadt von Rudolf von Habsburg die Reichsunmittelbarkeit. Blütezeit von Gewerbe im Mittelalter, Zerstörung durch Religionskriege, dann Stagnation und einmal an Bayern, einmal an Württemberg abgetreten. Nun wieder bayrische Großstadt. Das im Zweiten Weltkrieg zerstörte Unwiederbringliche im mittelalterlichen Stadtbild ist durch Modernes ersetzt.

GERMANY. ULM. 1959.

The cathedral is the religious building with the highest tower in Europe: It took nearly 200 years to build it (1377-1533). A gargoyle shares the view of the city and the Danube river.

This place on the river has been settled since the early Stone Age by Celts, Alemanic and Frankish tribes. In 1274 Rudolf of Habsburg declared the city to be subject to the emperor only. In the Middle Ages trade flourished, followed by destruction during religious wars, by stagnation and cessation once to Bavaria, then to Württemberg. Now Regensburg is again a Bavarian city; the Medieval architecture, irreparably destroyed by the bombs of the Second World War, has been replaced by modern structures.

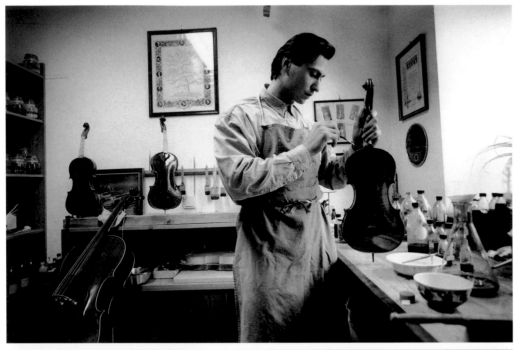

DEUTSCHLAND. REGENSBURG. 1995.

Oben: Thomas Goldfuss, dritte Generation der Geigenmacher-
familie Goldfuss, am Werk.

Unten: In einem Kellergewölbe im Dom singen sich die
Domspatzen für das Sonntagmorgenkonzert ein.

GERMANY. REGENSBURG. 1995.

Top: Thomas Goldfuss, third generation of the Goldfuss family of
violin makers in his workshop.

Bottom: The boy's choir of the cathedral rehearses before the
Sunday morning concert in a vault in the cathedral.

DEUTSCHLAND. REGENSBURG. 1995.

Statue von Don Juan de Austria, Sohn Kaiser Karls des V. und der Regensburger Handwerkertochter Barbara Blomberg. 1547 geboren, wird er 1571 als Sieger über die Türken in der Seeschlacht von Lepanto zum "Retter Europas" erklärt.

GERMANY. REGENSBURG. 1995.

Statue of Don Juan de Austria, son of Emperor Charles V and Barbara Blomberg, daughter of a Regensburg tradesman. Born in 1547, he was declared "Saviour of Europe" after his victory over the Turks in 1571 in the sea battle of Lepanto.

DEUTSCHLAND. KELHEIM. 1959.

Die Befreiungshalle. 34 Viktorien in Marmor - für die 34 deutschen Staaten - bilden einen Kreis und halten zwischen sich 17 Tafeln mit den Namen der Schlachten in den siegreichen Freiheitskriegen gegen Napoleon 1813 bis 1815.

GERMANY. KELHEIM. 1959.

"Liberation Hall": 34 Victories in marble - one for each of the German states - form a circle, holding between them 17 tablets inscribed with the names of the battles fought in the victorious War of Liberation against Napoleon from 1813-1815.

DEUTSCHLAND. DONAUSTAUF. 1959.
Blick auf die Walhalla vom gegenüberliegenden Donauufer. Im Inneren des nach dem Vorbild griechischer Tempel 1842 von Ludwig I. von Bayern errichteten Gebäudes sind weiße Marmorbüsten "rühmlich ausgezeichneter Teutscher" angebracht.

GERMANY. DONAUSTAUF. 1959.
View towards the Walhalla on the opposite bank of the Danube. Inside the Greek Revival building, erected in 1842 under Ludwig I of Bavaria, white marble busts "of praiseworthy and distinguished Germans" line the walls row upon row.

DEUTSCHLAND. ZWIEFALTEN. 1959.

Links: Eine Nonne schmückt einen Altar in der ehemaligen Abteikirche, einem der schönsten Barockbauten Deutschlands.

DEUTSCHLAND. WELTENBURG. 1995.

Rechts: Dampferfahrt durch den Donaudurchbruch von Kelheim zum Benediktinerkloster Weltenburg.

GERMANY. ZWIEFALTEN. 1959.

Left: A nun decorates an altar inside the church of the former abbey, one of the most beautiful German Barock buildings.

GERMANY. WELTENBURG. 1995.

Right: Steamboat ride from Kelheim to Weltenburg monastery through the Danube gorges.

DEUTSCHLAND. WELTENBURG. 1994.
Heiligenstatue vor dem Eingang zum Innenhof, in dem von
Mönchen gebrautes Bier ausgeschenkt wird.

GERMANY. WELTENBURG. 1994.
Statue of a saint at the entrance of the inner court of the
Benedictine monastery, where a special beer, brewed by the monks,
is served.

DEUTSCHLAND. BOGENBERG. 1959.
Links: Blick auf die Donau vom Marien-Wallfahrtsort.

GERMANY. BOGENBERG. 1959.
Left: View of the Danube from the place of pilgrimage.

DEUTSCHLAND. PASSAU. 1993.
Oben: Spazierweg von der Veste Oberhaus in die Stadt.

GERMANY. PASSAU. 1993.
Top: Walkway from the "Upper Fortress" to town.

DEUTSCHLAND. PASSAU. 1993.
Oben: Im alten Scharfrichterhaus der Stadt gibt es neue Bewohner: Künstler, die frische Luft ins Etablierte bringen. Edgar Liegel, Gründer des Kabaretts im Scharfrichterhaus.
Unten: Szene mit Sigi Zimmerschied, dem brillanten Komödianten und Mitglied des Kabaretts.

GERMANY. PASSAU. 1993.
Top: The old hangman's house has new inhabitants: mostly artists who love to rock the establishment. Edgar Liegel, founder of the "Cabaret in the Hangman's House".
Bottom: Scene with Sigi Zimmerschied, brilliant comedian and member of the cabaret.

DEUTSCHLAND. PASSAU. 1993.

Die Stadt ist auf der Landzunge am Zusammenfluß der drei Flüsse Inn, Donau und Ilz entstanden. Hier mischen sich ihre grünen, graublau und bräunlich gefärbten Gewässer und fließen, als Donau vereint über die deutsche Grenze nach Österreich.

GERMANY. PASSAU. 1993.

The city developed upon the spit of land at the confluence of three rivers: the Inn, the Danube und the Ilz. From here their green, grey-blue and brownish waters flow, united as the Danube, over the German border into Austria.

43

ÖSTERREICH. DAMPFERFAHRT
VON PASSAU NACH LINZ. 1993.
    Zwei Stunden Fahrt durch bewaldete Täler. Im Lautsprecher erklärt eine Frauenstimme Geographisches und erzählt Donaulegenden.

AUSTRIA. STEAMSHIP RIDE
FROM PASSAU TO LINZ. 1993.
    Two hours of gliding through wooded hills and valleys; over the loudspeaker a woman's voice explains geographical facts and tells Danube legends.

ÖSTERREICH. 1993.
Auf der österreichischen Donau sind acht Staustufen zu überwinden. Zwei weitere befinden sich im Bau.

AUSTRIA. 1993.
In Austria the Danube runs through eight locks, two more are being built.

ÖSTERREICH. MAUTHAUSEN. 1958.

Rechts: Schiffsglocke der Fähre über die Donau an dem Ort,
hinter dem unter Hitler ein Konzentrationslager Tausende von Opfern
forderte. Erhaltene Baracken, Wachtürme, Treppen, Steinbruch und
Monumente mit den Namen der Opfer dienen als Gedenk- und
Mahnmal.

AUSTRIA. MAUTHAUSEN. 1958.

Right: Ship's bell of the ferry across the Danube to the little town
behind which, in Hitler's time, a concentration camp demanded
thousands of victims. Some barracks, watchtowers, the huge steps
leading to the entrance, the deadly quarry, and monuments with the
names of the victims remain as a warning memorial.

ÖSTERREICH. SCHLOSS PERSENBEUG. 1993.

Links: Der Brunnen mit der Statue einer badenden Mutter im
Schloßpark ist einer der Lieblingsplätze des jetzigen Schloßherrn Erz-
herzog Dr. Michael Salvator Habsburg-Lothringen und seiner Gattin.

AUSTRIA. CASTLE OF PERSENBEUG. 1993.

Left: The fountain in the park of the castle, dominated by the
sculpture of a bathing mother, is one of the favourite spots of its
present inhabitants, Archduke Dr. Michael Salvator Habsburg-
Lothringen and his wife.

ÖSTERREICH. FAHRT DURCH DIE WACHAU. 1994.
38 Kilometer lang, eine der schönsten Donaulandschaften.

AUSTRIA. TRIP THROUGH THE WACHAU. 1994.
38 kilometers long, this is one of the most beautiful and fertile regions along the Danube.

ÖSTERREICH. 1958.
Fähre über die Donau bei Krems.

AUSTRIA. 1958.
Ferry across the Danube, near Krems.

ÖSTERREICH. WILLENDORF. 1994.

Die Venus von Willendorf, eine 11 cm große Figur aus Kalkstein, ist jetzt im Naturhistorischen Museum in Wien zu sehen. So steht nun eine stark vergrößerte Kopie ihrer üppigen Formen in einem Park nahe der Fundstelle und blickt auf die Donau im Tal.

AUSTRIA. WILLENDORF. 1994.

The Venus of Willendorf, an 11 centimeter high statuette, is now in Vienna's Museum of Natural History. Now a very enlarged copy of her ample forms in a park next to the place of her discovery, overlooking the Danube.

ÖSTERREICH. GREIN. 1994.

Oben: Im Café Blumensträußl ist die Einrichtung bis auf die Espressomaschine pures Biedermeier.

ÖSTERREICH. BURG CLAM. 1994

Unten: Eine der bedeutendsten österreichischen Burgen, die heute noch bewohnt werden. Johann August Strindberg lebte zwei Jahre lang in der Nähe und schrieb in dieser Zeit "Inferno" und "Reise nach Damaskus". Nun sitzt er als Wachsfigur hinter dem Schreibtisch in einem Burggemach.

AUSTRIA. GREIN. 1994.

Top: In the Café Blumensträussl everything but the espresso mashine is genuine Biedermeier.

AUSTRIA. CLAM CASTLE. 1994.

Bottom: This is one of the few fully intact Austrian fortresses, owned and inhabited since over 500 years by the Clam family. The Swedish writer August Strindberg lived nearby for two years, in which he wrote "Inferno" and "Trip to Damascus". Now he sits as a wax figure behind a desk in the castle.

ÖSTERREICH. SPITZ. 1993.
Am Fuß eines der Altäre der Pfarrkirche des Hl. Mauritius kündet ein Riesenkürbis das Erntedankfest an.

AUSTRIA. SPITZ. 1993.
A giant pumpkin, placed at the foot of one of the altars in the church of St. Mauritius announces the celebration of harvest thanksgiving.

ÖSTERREICH. GREIN. 1994.

Der barocke Engel schwebt über der geschnitzten Ölberggruppe an der Nordseite der Stadtpfarrkirche St. Ägyd.

AUSTRIA. GREIN. 1994.

The Barock angel floats above a group of carved figures of Christ and his disciples on the Mount of Olives on the north wall of the church of St. Ägyd.

ÖSTERREICH. MARIA TAFERL. 1959.
Souvenirstand in dem großen, der Heiligen Jungfrau Maria gewidmeten Wallfahrtsort.

AUSTRIA. MARIA TAFERL. 1959.
Stand with souvenirs in the big place of pilgrimage dedicated to the Virgin Mary.

ÖSTERREICH. MARIA TAFERL. 1993.
Oben: Dekoration auf einem Touristenbus.
ÖSTERREICH. WEISSENKIRCHEN. 1994.
Unten: Kirtag. Der Fleischhauer betätigt sich als Würstlbrater.

AUSTRIA. MARIA TAFERL. 1993.
Top: Decoration on a tourist bus.
AUSTRIA. WEISSENKIRCHEN. 1994.
Bottom: On the day of the church fair, the owner of the butcher shop fries his sausages on an outdoor grill.

ÖSTERREICH. MAUTERN. 1994.
Die Meisterköchin und Kochbuchautorin Liesl Wagner-Bacher auf
Hochtouren in der Küche ihres Hotels.

AUSTRIA. MAUTERN. 1994.
Liesl Wagner-Bacher, much decorated chef and cookbook author,
in full swing in the kitchen of her hotel.

ÖSTERREICH. MARIA LANZENDORF. 1961.
Meine Eltern beim Backhendlessen.

AUSTRIA. MARIA LANZENDORF. 1961.
My parents eating Viennese fried chicken.

ÖSTERREICH. DONAU BEI KREMS. 1994.
Rechts: Sie kamen mit ihrem eigenen Transportmittel vom anderen Ufer.

AUSTRIA. THE DANUBE NEAR KREMS. 1994.
Right: They came from the opposite shore by their own means of transport.

ÖSTERREICH. DÜRNSTEIN. 1958.
Links: In der Burg hoch über der Donau saß König Richard Löwenherz von 1192 bis 1193 gefangen. Der Kreuzritterweg nach Jerusalem folgte dem Fluß auf langen Strecken.

AUSTRIA. DÜRNSTEIN. 1958.
Left: In the fortress high above the Danube, King Richard the Lionhearted sat imprisoned from 1192-1193. The roads that the crusaders took on their ways to Jerusalem often followed long stretches of the Danube.

ÖSTERREICH. DÜRNSTEIN. 1994.
Blick auf einen der schönsten Orte der Wachau.

AUSTRIA. DÜRNSTEIN. 1994.
View of one of the most beautiful places in the Wachau region.

ÖSTERREICH. WIEN. 1961.
Weinlese in den Hügeln, durch sie fließt die Donau in die
österreichische Hauptstadt.

AUSTRIA. VIENNA. 1961.
Grape harvest in the vineyards through which the Danube makes
its way into the Austrian capital.

ÖSTERREICH. WIEN. 1958.
Links: Der Donaukanal. Der Fluß fließt außerhalb der Stadt.

AUSTRIA. VIENNA. 1958.
Left: The Danube Canal. The big river flows outside the capitol.

ÖSTERREICH. WIEN. 1975.
Oben: Ein Fiaker wartet auf eine Fuhre.

AUSTRIA. VIENNA. 1975.
Top: The driver feeds the pigeons while waiting for a customer.

ÖSTERREICH. WIEN. 1980.
Concordia-Ball im großen Saal des Rathauses.

AUSTRIA. VIENNA. 1980.
Concordia Ball in the great hall of the town hall.

ÖSTERREICH. LOBAU. 1994.
  Tanzlokal "Der Rote Hiasl" an den Ufern der Neuen Donau
bei Wien.

AUSTRIA. LOBAU. 1994.
  Dancefloor at the "Der Rote Hiasl" restaurant, near the banks of
the New Danube, just outside Vienna.

ÖSTERREICH. LOBAU. 1959.
Zahlkellner. Er hatte schon viele Male "Komme sofort" versichert. Nun ist er da, über alle Vorwürfe erhaben.

AUSTRIA. LOBAU. 1959.
Headwaiter. He had already announced his immediate arrival many a time. Finally he materialises, beyond any possibility of reproach.

ÖSTERREICH. WIEN. 1980.
Die Burgschauspielerin Erika Pluhar singt für ihre Freunde in einer Buschenschenke beim Heurigen.

AUSTRIA. VIENNA. 1980.
The actress Erika Pluhar sings for her friends at a "Heurigen", a restaurant where a bunch of branches above the door announces the new wine.

ÖSTERREICH. WIEN. 1994.
Links: Ulrike Truger vor ihrer Skulptur "Große Schreitende".

AUSTRIA. VIENNA. 1994.
Left: Ulrike Truger infront of her sculpture, "Striding Woman".

ÖSTERREICH. WIEN. 1961.
Oben: Kinder baden in den Lacken in den Praterauen.

AUSTRIA. VIENNA. 1961.
Top: Children bathe in the ponds of the Prater meadows.

ÖSTERREICH. DER HELDENBERG. 1975.
Hier liegt der Feldmarschall Radetzky begraben und eine große Anzahl von Büsten, arrangiert um Rondelle und in Alleen, erinnert an militärische Helden der Habsburgerzeit.

AUSTRIA. MOUNT OF THE HEROES. 1975.
Burial place of Fieldmarshall Count Radetzky. The memorial near Viennas also consists of a Greek Revival temple and a great number of busts representing military heroes of the Habsburg times, arranged in circles and along alleyways.

ÖSTERREICH. WIEN. 1959.
Friedhof der Namenlosen. Das gleiche gußeiserne Kruzifix schmückt das Grab aller, die sich in der Donau ertränkt haben oder in ihr ertrunken sind und namenlos blieben.

AUSTRIA. VIENNA. 1959.
Cemetery of the Nameless. The same cast-iron crucifix adorns the tombs of all those who drowned themselves in the Danube or remained nameless after perishing in the river.

ÖSTERREICH. DER BRAUNSBERG. 1958.

Von hier hat man einen Blick auf drei Grenzen, die alle der Donau entlanglaufen: Der Berg ist in Österreich, links im Hintergrund beginnt die Slowakei und rechts Ungarn.

AUSTRIA. THE BRAUNSBERG. 1958.

From here, one sees three borders running along the Danube: the hill is in Austria, in the background on the left begins Slovakia, on the right Hungary.

SLOWAKEI. BRATISLAVA. 1993.
Oben: Wachablöse vor dem Eingang zum Schloß der slowakischen Hauptstadt.
Unten: Barockbrunnen und moderne Donaubrücke.

SLOWAKIA. BRATISLAVA. 1993.
Top: Changing of the Guards in front of the entrance to the castle above the Slovak capitol.
Bottom: Barock fountain and modern bridge spanning the Danube.

ÖSTERREICH. KITTSEE. 1958.
Knapp hinter den österreichischen Kühen verläuft die
slowakische Grenze. Im Hintergrund das Schloß von Bratislava.

AUSTRIA. KITTSEE. 1958.
A short distance behind the Austrian cows is the Slowak border.
In the background, the Castle of Bratislava.

UNGARN. UNGARISCHE GRENZE. 1994.
Lokale Spezialitäten

HUNGARY. HUNGARIAN BORDER. 1994.
Tempting displays of local specialities.

UNGARN. GYÖR. 1993.

Vier Flüsse fließen in dieser Stadt zusammen: die Raab, die Rábca, die Marcal und die Mosoner Donau. Györ ist seit der Steinzeit besiedelt, wurde von Stefan dem Heiligen zu einem der 10 ungarischen Bistümer ernannt, bietet reizende Gänge entlang zahlreicher Uferpromenaden und farbenfreudige barocke Architektur.

HUNGARY. GYÖR. 1993.

Four rivers: the Raab, the Rábca, the Marcal and the Moson Danube meet in this town. The place has been settled since the Stone Age. Hungary's Saint Stephen named it one of the ten bishoprics of the country. It offers charming walks along its many river banks and colourful Barock architecture.

UNGARN. VISEGRÁD. 1993.

Ort mit 2000-jähriger Geschichte hoch über dem Donauknie im Komitat Pest. Die Slawen, die den Römern folgten, gaben ihm den Namen Visegrád: Hohe Burg.

HUNGARY. VISEGRÁD. 1993.

High above a mighty bend in the Danube the ruins of Visegrád - high Fortress - dominate the landscape. Their history goes back 2000 years, the Slavic tribes, who followed the Romans, gave it its present name.

UNGARN. SZENTENDRE. 1993.

Ungarns Montmartre, 20 Kilometer stromaufwärts vom Zentrum von Budapest entfernt. Viele Künstler leben hier. Überall werden die farbenfrohen Stickereien der Frauen von Szentendre und Umgebung zum Kauf angeboten.

HUNGARY. SZENTENDRE. 1993.

The "Hungarian Montmartre" is situated 20 kilometers upstream from the center of Budapest. Many artists live and work here. Everywhere the colourful embroideries of the women of Szentendre and surroundings are offered for sale.

UNGARN. BUDAPEST. 1994.

Linke Seite: Blick von Buda auf den am anderen Ufer der Donau liegenden Stadtteil Pest: magische Anziehungskraft des Panoramas der Stadt, die diesen Fluß am schönsten einrahmt.

HUNGARY. BUDAPEST. 1994.

Left Page: View from Buda towards Pest, across the Danube: magical attraction by the panorama of the city that most perfectly frames this river.

UNGARN. BUDAPEST. 1993.

Links: Der Schriftsteller Miklos Vamos im Café New York.
Rechts: Budapest. 1993. Eingang zu einem der zahlreichen kleinen Restaurants in der Váci Utca.

HUNGARY. BUDAPEST. 1993.

Left: The writer Miklos Vamos at a table in the Café New York
Right: Budapest. 1993. Entrance to one of the numerous little restaurants in the Váci Utca.

UNGARN. RACKEVE. 1994.

Ein Mann fischt in der Donau vor der für den Prinzen Eugen von Savoyen gebauten Sommerresidenz, in der sich der Prinz wahrscheinlich nie aufhielt.

HUNGARY. RACKEVE. 1994.

A man is fishing in the Danube in front of the summer residence built for Prince Eugene of Savoy, who probably never stayed in it.

UNGARN. MOHÁCS. 1994.
Anlegestelle der Donaufähre. Nur ein paar Kilometer von der einstigen jugoslawischen Grenze entfernt, war die kleine Stadt einst ein wichtiger Donauhafen.

HUNGARY. MOHÁCS. 1994.
Stop for the ferry across the Danube, a few kilometers away from the former Yugoslav border. Mohács was once an important Danube port.

ÖSTERREICH. 1994.
AUS DEM BERICHT ÜBER DIE BOSNISCHE
FLÜCHTLINGSFAMILIE VON IHRER
BETREUERIN MARIA LOLEY:

"Der Vater der bosnischen Flüchtlingsfamilie heißt Softic Meho, seine Frau heißt Fehima. Sie wohnen in der Ortschaft Föllim, die zur Gemeinde Poysdorf gehört.

Der Mann ist nach Österreich gekommen, um sich nach einem möglichen Aufenthaltsort für seine Familie umzusehen, da ein Kriegsausbruch sich bereits abgezeichnet hat. Er hatte in Österreich einen Verwandten, der als Gastarbeiter beschäftigt war und den er besuchte. Bereits wenige Tage nach seiner Ankunft in Österreich brach der Krieg aus, seine Heimat Nordbosnien wurde der erste Kriegsschauplatz. Der Mann konnte nicht mehr zurück, auch konnte er keine Nachricht von sich geben. Dadurch mußten sich seine Angehörigen alleine auf die Flucht machen.

Von dieser Familie sind die Frau, drei Kinder, die Großeltern mit ein paar anderen Verwandten und Bekannten auf der Flucht gewesen. Sie flohen wochenlang durch Wälder, schliefen im Freien und in Erdlöchern, ständig in Gefahr, von den Serben entdeckt zu werden. Ein naher Verwandter, ein 15-jähriger Bub, wurde auf dieser Flucht durch eine Tschetnik-Patrouille von einer solchen Granate tödlich getroffen.

Durch die Entbehrungen der drei Wochen langen Flucht hat der Großvater 20 Kilo verloren. Die Familie ist total erschöpft in der Nacht in Österreich angekommen, der Großvater wurde sofort in ein Spital eingeliefert, starb aber schon 14 Tage später an den Folgen der Entbehrungen.

Nicht lange nach Ankunft der Familie erkrankte der Mann und Familienerhalter schwer am Herz, benötigte eine Herzoperation und ist in der Folge arbeitsunfähig. Derzeit muß die Familie von einem minimalen Geld von 1500 österreichischen Schilling pro Person im Monat leben. Aber zwei der Söhne haben einen Lehrplatz, wodurch sie die Familie wesentlich miterhalten. Die Mitarbeiter der Flüchtlingshilfe Poysdorf helfen in der Betreuung.

Die Perspektive der Familie ist natürlich sehr schlecht. Sie wissen inzwischen, daß ihr Haus in Nordbosnien nicht mehr steht und daß vor allem die Älteren nicht zurückkehren können."

AUSTRIA. 1994.
FROM THE REPORT OF MARIA LOLEY,
REFUGEE AID WORKER IN POYSDORF
ABOUT THE SOFTIC FAMILY:

"The name of the Bosnian family is Softic, Meho (the man) and Fehime (the wife): They live in Foellim, part of Poysdorf commune.

The man came to Austria looking for a possible place of refuge for his family, everything foreboding war at home. He visited a relative, who worked as a guestworker in Austria. A few days after his arrival in Austria war broke out; the first hostilities took place in his homeland, northern Bosnia. His family had to flee on their own, the man could not return or take up contact.

The family members taking flight were the wife, the three children, the grandparents, joined by a couple of relatives and friends. For several weeks they walked and hid in forests, spent nights in holes dug in the earth, in constant danger of being caught by the Serbs. One close relative, a 15 year old boy, was hit and died on his flight.

The grandfather lost over 40 pounds due to the deprivations of the flight. Finally they arrived in Austria, totally exhausted, in the middle of the night. The grandfather was hospitalised at once, but died 2 weeks later from exhaustion.

During the first year in Austria, two families had to share the small house that luckily was quickly found. From the start, the local population was very helpful, calling the arrivals "our refugees".

Then serious heart disease struck the father and provider of the family. He had to have open heart surgery and has not been able to work since. At this point, the family has to live with the minimum of 1500 Austrian shillings per person per month. But the two older sons found places as mechanics' apprentices and help considerably. The family is also looked after by the Refugee Aid of Poysdorf.

The outlook for the future of the family is naturally bleak. They know now that their house in northern Bosnia has been destroyed and that the older members of the family will probably not be able to return. Moreover, there is little chance for the parents to find work in Austria. This causes many depressions, which they have a tendency to hide. The children have assimilated themselves and count on building a future in Austria."

ÖSTERREICH. FÖLLIM. 1994.
Eine Familie von Moslemflüchtlingen aus Bosnien in ihrer Küche mit Maria Loley (zweite von links).

AUSTRIA. FÖLLIM. 1994.
Family of Bosnian Muslim refugees in their kitchen with Maria Loley (second from left).

JUGOSLAWIEN. DIE DONAU BEI SMEDEREVO. 1958.
Kinder spielen auf den Ruinen der Festungsmauer.

YUGOSLAVIA. THE DANUBE AT SMEDEREVO. 1958.
Boys play on top of the ruined walls of the former fortress.

JUGOSLAWIEN. AVALA. 1958.
16 Kilometer südlich von Belgrad liegt der Avala-Hügel, auf dessen Gipfel Ivan Mestrovic' monumentales "Grabmal des Unbekannten Soldaten" steht.

YUGOSLAVIA. AVALA. 1958.
16 kilometers south of Belgrade stands the hill of Avala, crowned by Ivan Mestrovic's monumental "Tomb of the Unknown Soldier".

JUGOSLAWIEN.
PEĆ. 1958.
Zwei Moslems beten vor
dem Mihrab in der alten
Moschee der Stadt.

YUGOSLAVIA.
PEĆ. 1958.
Two Moslems say prayers in
front of the Mihrab in the old
mosque.

JUGOSLAWIEN. NOVI PAZAR. 1958.
Hutgeschäft.

YUGOSLAVIA. NOVI PAZAR. 1958.
Hat shop.

JUGOSLAWIEN. PARAĆIN. 1958.
Links: Bauernmarkt. an der Morava.

YUGOSLAVIA. PARAĆIN. 1958.
Left: Peasant market on the banks of the Morava river.

JUGOSLAWIEN. SMEDEREVO. 1958.
Oben: Im Hintergrund die Türme der Festung Smederevo.

YUGOSLAVIA. SMEDEREVO. 1958.
Top: In the background are the towers of the fortress.

JUGOSLAWIEN.
NOVI PAZAR.
1958.
Straßenszene.

YUGOSLAVIA.
NOVI PAZAR.
1958.
Street scene.

JUGOSLAWIEN. SOPOČANI. 1958.
Eines der byzantinischen Klöster mit wunderbaren Fresken, die südlich der Donau liegen.

YUGOSLAVIA. SOPOČANI. 1958.
One of the Byzantine monasteries, famous for their frescoes, situated south of the Danube.

JUGOSLAWIEN. DAMPFER. 1958.

Zweimal in der Woche fuhr das Boot um acht Uhr abends von Belgrad ab und kam am nächsten Tag um zwei Uhr nachmittags in dem modernen serbischen Hafenort Kladovo, zehn Kilometer südlich des Eisernen Tores, an.

Auf dem Boot gab es eine Kabine erster und zwei Kabinen zweiter Klasse, der Rest der zahlreichen Passagiere verbrachte die Nacht zwischen ihren Säcken und Körben. Auf dem unteren Deck wimmelte es von Gänsen, Hühnern und Schafen. Ich verbrachte die Nacht auf einem Stuhl, bis mich bei Sonnenaufgang ein Uniformierter in eine Toilette einsperrte, weil ich das Felsendefilee von Kazan vor dem Eisernen Tor zu fotografieren anfing. Natürlich gab es Postkarten jenes Panoramas auf dem Schiff zu kaufen.

1971 sind die Insel Ada Kaleh und die Felswände des Eisernen Tores dem Bau des großen Kraftwerkes zum Opfer gefallen.

YUGOSLAVIA. STEAMBOAT. 1958.

In 1958 this was a Yugoslav steamer. The boat left Belgrade twice a week at 8 pm and arrived the next day at 2 pm in the port of Kladovo, ten kilometers south of the Iron Gate, which gained great importance after the building of the hydroelectric station in 1971

The boat was overcrowded. There were one first class and two second class cabins, both occupied. The rest of the numerous passengers spent the night between their sacks and baskets. On the lower deck geese, chicken and sheep competed for space. I sat on a chair until, at sunrise, when I got up to photograph the splendid rock defile of Kazan leading to the Iron Gate, a man in uniform said that this was forbidden and locked me into one of the toilets. He was not to be convinced that postcards of the same panorama could be bought everywhere.

The island of Ada Kaleh and the Rocks of Kazan fell victim to the building of the hydroelectric dam.

JUGOSLAWIEN. LANDSCHAFT ZWISCHEN STUDENITZA UND NOVI PAZAR. 1958.

YUGOSLAVIA. LANDSCAPE BETWEEN STUDENICA AND NOVI PAZAR. 1958.

RUMÄNIEN. ORŞOVA. 1994.

Unter der riesigen Wasserfläche liegt die Stadt Orşova, kurz nach der Eroberung Dakiens durch den römischen Kaiser Trajan gegründet. 1971 wird die Stadt durch den rumänisch-jugoslawischen Stauseebau am Eisernen Tor überflutet.

RUMANIA. ORŞOVA. 1994.

Under the huge surface of water lies Orşova. In 1971 the city was flooded because of the creation of the Iron Gate dam. A new town now borders the new lake.

RUMÄNIEN. BĂILE HERCULANE. 1994.

Heiße Quellen, die schon den Römern bekannt waren, entspringen in den Bergen nördlich von Turnu Severin. Ihre Heilkraft und die schöne Umgebung haben jahrhundertelang Besucher angezogen.

RUMANIA. BĂILE HERCULANE. 1994.

The hot springs emerging in the mountains north of Drobeta Turnu Severin were already known to the Romans. A spa grew up in "Hercules' Bath", the healing powers of the waters and the lovely surroundings attracted many visitors.

RUMÄNIEN. ORĂŞTIE. 1958.

Auf dem Weg nach Grădishtea Muncelului, der Festung des Dakerkönigs Decebal, und den Goldminen in Roşia Montana, hinter denen Trajan und seine römischen Legionen her waren.

Die Landschaft ist einsam. Ein Mann in Lokaltracht taucht auf, und wir fragen nach dem Weg. "Grădistea Muncelului", sagt er, "das ist einfach. Sie fahren nach rechts und folgen den Telegrafenmasten." Wir biegen von der Straße auf einen Feldweg ab, ohne zu überlegen, daß er selbst wahrscheinlich nie in einem Auto gefahren ist. Unser Jeep rutscht, bleibt stecken, fährt durch Bergbäche. Ein Schafhirte, der unsere Manöver beobachtet, klärt die Sache: Gradistea Muncelului kann man nur mit einem Holztransport erreichen, die Reise auf dem offenen Güterwagen dauert einen Tag und der Zug fährt selten.

In den Mauerresten sind Zeichen der Schlachten sichtbar: die Daker versuchten, die von den Römern geschlagenen Breschen mit Säulenresten zu reparieren.

RUMANIA. ORĂŞTIE. 1958.

En route to Grădishtea Muncelului, fortress of the Dacian King Decebal, and the gold mines of Roşia Montana, one of the major goals of Trajan's legions.

We drive through a lonely landscape, no map indicates the way. A man in local dress shows up who seems to know. "Grădistea Muncelului?", he thinks for a moment. "That's easy. Just get off the big road to the right and follow the telephone poles." We follow his advice, turn onto the dirt road without thinking that he probably never drove a car. Our jeep slides, gets stuck, overcomes huge bumps, boulders, mountain brooks. A shepherd who has been watching our manoeuvres explains: "The only way to get to the mountain fortress is with a freight train, transporting wood. The trip lasts a day and the train runs very infrequently.

Higher up, overlooking the valley, are the remains of four square watchtowers, one at each corner of the fortress. The crumbling walls retain battlescars: the Dacians stuck pieces of columns in the breeches caused by Roman attacks - but they could not hold the fortress.

RUMÄNIEN. ROȘIA MONTANA. 1958.

"Die Festung", wie die Leute von Roșia Montana den Berg mit den ehemaligen Goldminen nennen, liegt nahe der kleinen Stadt. Nur eine riesige Steinwand steht noch, in ihr klaffen die Öffnungen der Schäfte. In ihrer unermüdlichen Suche nach Gold fanden die Einwohner Skelette römischer Sklaven, die zur Arbeit in den Minen verurteilt waren, die Fußfessel noch um die Knöchel.

RUMANIA. ROȘIA MONTANA. 1958.

"The Fortress", as the inhabitants of Roșia Montana call the mountain that contained the gold mines, is not far from the small town. It is hollowed out now, a huge shell of rock, the former mine shafts just gaping holes. In their never ending search for gold the people of Rosia Montana came across skeletons of Roman slaves, condemned to work in the mines, iron fetters still around the bones of their ankles.

RUMÄNIEN. OLT-FLUSS. 1958.
Links: Der Olt-Fluß mündet in die Donau.

RUMANIA. OLT RIVER. 1958.
Left: The Olt river flows into the danube.

RUMÄNIEN. OLTENIEN. 1958.
Oben: Eine Drei-Männer-Kapelle auf der Fahrt nach Răşinari.

RUMANIA. OLTENIA. 1958.
Top: A three-man-band on the way to Răşinari.

RUMÄNIEN. RĂȘINARI. 1958.
Bauernhochzeit. Die meisten Gäste tragen ihre Trachten. Offiziell geheiratet wird am ersten Tag, aber die Festlichkeiten enden erst am Abend des dritten.

RUMANIA. RĂȘINARI. 1958.
Peasant wedding. Most of the guests wear their national costume. The official wedding takes place on the first day, but the festivities continue to the end of the third.

RUMÄNIEN. SIEBENBÜRGEN. 1958.

Ein frisch verlobtes Mädchen, feierlich angezogen, mit Brautkrone, geht mit zwei Freundinnen von Haus zu Haus, um das große Ereignis anzukündigen. Ihr Gesicht erinnerte mich an eines, das ich in dem spätgotischen geschnitzten Chorgestühl des Ulmer Doms gesehen hatte - einer der Städte, von denen ihre Vorfahren die Donau hinunter ausgezogen sein könnten.

RUMANIA. TRANSYLVANIA. 1958.

A newly engaged girl, dressed in her Sunday costume and wearing a bridal crown, walks with two girl friends from house to house to announce the great event. Her face made me think of another one I saw: a wooden sculpture in the Gothic pews of Ulm cathedral - the city from which the girl's ancestors could have set out down the Danube to Transylvania.

RUMÄNIEN. TURNU SEVERIN. 1994.
Links: Ein herrenloses Pferd vor dem Opernhaus.

RUMANIA. TURNU SEVERIN. 1994.
Left: A loose horse in front of the opera house.

RUMÄNIEN. TURNU SEVERIN. 1994.
Fußballmatch am Fuß eines Monumentes.

RUMANIA. TURNU SEVERIN. 1994.
Soccer match at the foot of a monument.

RUMÄNIEN. TURNU SEVERIN. 1994.
Empfangsdame im Parkhotel.

RUMANIA. TURNU SEVERIN. 1994.
Receptionist in the Park Hotel.

RUMÄNIEN. BEI SIMIAN. 1994.
Unermüdliche Fischer stehen stundenlang im Wasser. Auf der anderen Seite des Flusses: Serbien.

RUMANIA. AT SIMIANA. 1994.
Undaunted fishermen stand for hours on rocks in the shallow waters near the river banks. The opposite bank belongs to Serbia.

BULGARIEN. BELOGRADČIK. 1994.
    Um von der bulgarischen Hauptstadt Sofia zum Donauhafen von Vidin zu gelangen, kann man den Weg durch die phantastische Felsenlandschaft von Belogradčik wählen. Im Herzen dieser Landschaft liegt die Festung Kaleto.

BULGARIA. BELOGRADČIK. 1994.
    Making a small detour from the highway leading from Sofia to the Danubian port of Vidin, one passes through the fantastic panorama of the rocks of Belogradčick. The bizarre stone columns shelter the fortress of Kaleto.

BULGARIEN. BELOGRADČIK. 1994.
Kleiner Laden im Zentrum der Stadt. Angeboten werden
Zwiebeln, Kartoffeln, Zitronen, ein großer Kohlkopf, etwas Obst.

BULGARIA. BELOGRADČIK. 1994.
Small shop in the center: it offers onions, potatoes, lemons, a big
head of cabbage and a bit of fruit.

BULGARIEN. SVIŠTOV. 1994.

Eines der rosa Häuser von Svistov spiegelt sich in der Fensterscheibe eines Cafés.

Svištov ist der drittwichtigste bulgarische Donauhafen nach Ruse und Lom. Die Stadt war ein Sitz der Ostgoten unter Theoderich, Militärbasis für Feldzüge gegen Awaren und Slawen. Sie war die wichtigste Festung im römischen Verteidigungssystem im Donauraum. Selbst unter den Türken war sie ein lebendiges Handelszentrum. 1877 überquerten auf einer vom rumänischen Zimnicea zum bulgarischen Svištov geschlagenen Pontonbrücke die ersten russischen und rumänischen Einheiten, die am Krieg gegen die Türken teilnahmen, die Donau. Heute wimmelt die Stadt, die eine große Universität hat, von Studenten.

BULGARIA. SVIŠTOV. 1994.

One of the pink houses of Svištov is reflected in the window of a café.

Among Bulgarian Danube ports Svistov holds third place, after Ruse and Lom. It was the seat of the Ostrogoths under Theoderich and military base for their campaigns against Avaric and Slavic tribes. Later, it was the most important link in the Roman defence system along the Danube. Even under Turkish occupation the city remained a lively center of trade. 1877 the first Russian and Rumanian troops crossed the Danube over a pontoon bridge from the Rumanian Zimnicea to the Bulgarian Svištov - at the beginning of the war against the Turks. It now is a lively university town.

BULGARIEN.
NIKOPOL. 1994.
    Drei junge Männer tauchen
auf und beobachten gespannt,
wie ich die frühmittelalterliche
Kirche von Peter und Paul
fotografiere. Sie wollen
Zigaretten; als Gegenleistung
stellen sie sich für meine
Kamera in Position.
    Nikopol ist in der Geschichte
berühmt, weil hier das
katholische Europa zum ersten
Mal den osmanischen Türken
Widerstand leistete. Eine stolze
Armee von Kreuzrittern,
bestehend aus Franzosen,
Venetianern, Burgundern,
Engländern, Ungarn und
Rumänen, wird hier am 25.
September 1396 von Sultan
Bayezid I. Yildirim vernichtend
geschlagen.

BULGARIA.
NIKOPOL. 1994.
    Three young men appear
and watch intently as I
photograph the early Medieval
church of Peter and Paul. They
want cigarettes. In return they
strike a pose for my camera.
    Nikopol has a name in
history: it was here that
Catholic Europe for the first
time put up a resistance against
the Osmanic Turks. A proud
army of crusaders, made up of
French, Venetians,
Burgundians, Englishmen,
Hungarians and Rumanians
was cruelly beaten by Sultan
Bayezid I Yildirim on
September 25th, 1396.

BULGARIEN. NIKOPOL. 1994.
Blick vom Hügel über der Stadt auf das am anderen Donau-Ufer
liegende rumänische Turnu Măgurele mit seiner riesigen, die
Umwelt verschmutzenden Kunstdüngerfabrik.

BULGARIA. NIKOPOL. 1994.
View from the hill above town towards the Rumanian town of
Turnu Măgurele and the huge, polluting, artificial fertilizer plant.

BULGARIEN. BELENE. 1994.

Die Wäscherinnen von Belene kommen mit ihren Ladungen von Leintüchern und Teppichen ans Donau-Ufer. Sie dreschen den Schmutz aus der eingeseiften, nassen Wäsche mit Holzflegeln heraus. Was sauber ist, wird in Plastik eingewickelt und auf dem Eselswagen zurücktransportiert. Im Hintergrund die Insel von Belene, die größte Insel Bulgariens.

Das kommunistische Regime hatte hier ein Arbeits- und Umerziehungslager angelegt.

BULGARIA. BELENE. 1994.

The washerwomen of Belene come to the bank of the Danube with their loads of linens and carpets. They use wooden flails to beat the dirt out of the wet, soapy wash. Rinsed and clean, all is rolled up in plastic sheets, and loaded onto the donkey cart to be driven back to town.

Under the communist regime a "Labour and Re-Education Camp" had been installed in Belene.

RUMÄNIEN. JURILOFKA. 1994.
Ein Fischerdorf südlich des Donaudeltas am Razim See, durch eine Landzunge vom Schwarzen Meer getrennt. Rechts im Hintergrund eine Fischkonservenfabrik.

RUMANIA. JURILOFKA. 1994.
A fishermen's village south of the Delta of the Danube, on the banks of Lake Razim, seperated by a land tongue from the Black Sea. In the background, on the right, a fish canning plant.

RUMÄNIEN. BORCEA. 1994.

Oben: Borcea ist ein Dorf am westlichen Arm der Donau, die kurz davor, nachdem sie 399 km lang die Grenze zwischen Rumänien und Bulgarien bildet, nach Norden in rein rumänisches Territorium abbiegt und auf 100 Kilometern in zwei Arme teilt.

Das Mädchen in der geblümten Schürze will wissen, ob wir Seife zu verkaufen haben, gibt sich aber dann mit einer Packung Kaffee zufrieden.

Unten: Der Fischer mit den zwei Booten in der Borcea Donau beklagt sich bitterlich über die Verschmutzung. "Die Abwässer rinnen in den Fluß, es gibt keine Regulierung, die Fische sterben."

RUMANIA. BORCEA. 1994.

Top: The village of Borcea is situated on the western arm of the Danube, which forms the frontier between Rumania and Bulgaria for 471 kilometers until it bends north, entirely onto Rumanian territory and splits for a distance of about a 100 kilometers into two arms.

The girl in the flowered apron comes to ask if we had soap for sale, but settled for the gift of a package of coffee.

Bottom: The fisherman, with his two boats anchored in the Borcea Danube, complains bitterly about the pollution. "The sewers run straight into the river, there are no regulations, the fish disappear and die."

RUMÄNIEN. CĂLARĂŞI. 1994.
Links: Am Borcea-Arm der Donau gelegener Getreidehafen.

RUMANIA. CĂLARĂŞI. 1994.
Left: On the Borcea arm of the Danube.

RUMÄNIEN. ADAMCLISI. 1994.
Das neu aufgebaute Tropaeum Traiani aus dem Jahr 108/109.

RUMANIA. ADAMCLISI. 1994.
The new erected Tropaeum Traiani monument from 108/109.

RUMÄNIEN. NAVODARI. 1994.
Auf der Straße von Tulcea nach Constanţa.

RUMÄNIEN. HISTRIA. 1994.
Rechts: Die Ruinen der griechischen Kolonie Histria.

RUMANIA. NAVODARI. 1994.
On the street leading from Constanţa to Tulcea.

RUMANIA. HISTRIA. 1994.
Right: The ruins of the Greek colony of Histria.

RUMÄNIEN. DER HAFEN VON TULCEA. 1994.
Hier ist das Tor des Donaudeltas, die Endstation für Auto-,
Eisenbahn- und Flugwege; jeder weitere Transport ist nur mehr auf
dem Wasser möglich.

RUMANIA. THE PORT OF TULCEA. 1994.
This is the gate to the Delta of the Danube, the end of all rail-
and roadways: all further transport proceeds by water.

RUMÄNIEN. TULCEA. 1994.
    Herr Constantin Acmoja. Er sitzt in seinem Büro vor einer großen Karte des Donaudeltas, dessen Touristenverkehr ihm untersteht.

RUMANIA. TULCEA. 1994.
    Mr. Constantin Acmoja sits in his office in front of a huge map of the Delta. He is the director of tourism of the entire region.

RUMÄNIEN. GALAŢI. 1958.

RUMANIA. GALAŢI. 1958.

RUMÄNIEN. JURILOFKA. 1958.
Rechts: Von Lippowanern geführter Teeladen.

RUMANIA. JURILOFKA. 1958.
Right: Teashop run by a Lipoveni fisherman.

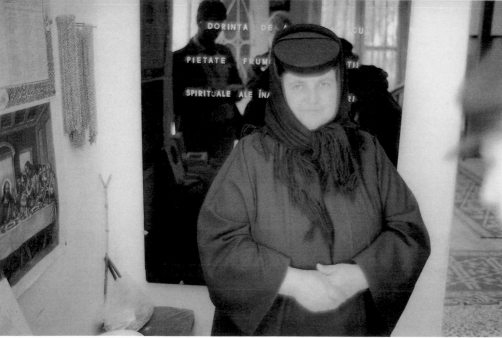

RUMÄNIEN. CELIC DERE. 1994.

Oben: Das Nonnenkloster liegt 29 Kilometer entfernt von Tulcea zwischen Hügeln mit Weingärten. Als wir ankommen, singen drei der achtzig Nonnen, die noch im Kloster leben, eine feierliche Abendandacht.

Unten: Die Schwester, die Besucher empfängt und das kleine Museum zeigt, ist stolz auf die ausgestellten, von den Nonnen angefertigten Stickereien, lokalen Teppiche und Ikonen. "Es ist sehr schön hier", bemerkt sie, "ich war einmal auf einer Reise in einer großen Stadt. Das genügt."

RUMANIA. MONASTERY OF CELIC DERE. 1994.

Top: The nunnery lies at a distance of 29 kilometers from Tulcea in rolling hills with vineyards. When we arrive, three of the 80 nuns who still live here, sing an evening mass.

Bottom: The nun who is in charge of receiving visitors and showing the little museum is especially proud of the chasubles and ornaments embroidered by the nuns, some local carpets and icons. "Isn't it beautiful here?", she says. "I once went on a trip to a big t own. That was quite enough."

RUMÄNIEN. JURILOFKA. 1994.

Haus einer lippowanischen Fischerfamilie. Als ich 1958 in
Jurilofka war, habe ich in einem solchen Haus übernachtet. Alles
war spiegelblank geputzt, die von der Hausfrau angefertigten
Stickereien bedeckten Tischtücher, Vorhänge und auch meinen
Kopfpolster. Ich verließ Jurilofka am nächsten Morgen mit einem in
die Wange gepreßten Kreuzstichmuster.

RUMANIA. JURILOFKA. 1994.

House of a Lipoveni fisherman's family. When I was here in 1958
I spent a night in such a house; inside everything was shining with
cleanliness, the embroideries, made by the woman of the house,
decorated tablecloths, curtains and even my pillow. Next morning I
left Jurilofka with a cross-stitch pattern etched into my cheek.

RUMÄNIEN. SULINA-KANAL. 1994.
Vorbeifahrende Frachter „bedrohen" unsere Schaluppe.

RUMANIA. ON THE SULINA CANAL. 1994.
From our small shaluppa passing freighters look menacing.

RUMÄNIEN. CRIŞEN. SULINA-KANAL. 1994.
Rechts: Links mündet die alte Donau in den Sulina-Kanal.

RUMANIA. CRIŞEN. SULINA CANAL. 1994.
Right: On the left a piece of the old Danube runs into the canal.

RUMÄNIEN. RAZIM SEE. 1958.

Die Frauen waschen in einem Seitenkanal, die Männer haben den Tag fischend auf dem Riesensee verbracht, nun haben sie auf ihrem Kutter Segel gesetzt, um die Heimkehr zu beschleunigen.

RUMANIA. LAKE RAZIM. 1958.

The women finish doing their laundry, the men have spent the day fishing on the lake, now they have set sails to speed up their return.

RUMÄNIEN. SULINA. 1994.
    Meer- und Binnenhafen, an der Schwarzmeermündung des
Sulina-Armes gelegen, der östlichste Punkt und die tiefstgelegene
Siedlung Rumäniens.

RUMANIA. SULINA. 1994.
    Inland and sea port, situated at the end of the Sulina Canal at
the Black Sea; the most eastern and lowest lying town of Rumania.

RUMÄNIEN. SULINA. 1994.
Oben: Der Koch im Hotel Sulina.
RUMÄNIEN. TULCEA. 1958.
Unten: Fischkonservenfabrik. Damals hieß sie "23. August",
zählte 250 Arbeiter. Unter anderem wurde Kaviar für den Export
produziert. Ob die Blume im Haar über die unbeschützten Hände
tröstete?

RUMANIA. SULINA. 1994.
Top: The cook of the Sulina Hotel.
RUMANIA. TULCEA. 1958.
Bottom: Fish cannery. It was named "23rd of August" and
employed 250 workers. Amongst the goods canned here was caviar
for export only. Did the girl with the unprotected hands find comfort
in the flower she stuck in her hair?

RUMÄNIEN. SULINA. 1994.

Lippowanischer Fischer vor dem Eingang zu seinem Haus. Die Lippowaner halten an ihren Bräuchen und langen weißen Bärten fest. Abends, wenn sie von einem Tag auf dem Wasser heimrudern, singen sie russische Lieder.

RUMANIA. SULINA. 1994.

Lipoveni fisherman at the entrance to his yard. The Lipoveni are Russians who fled their homeland for religious reasons in the 19th century. They settled in the Delta and still provide most of the fishermen. They stick to their customs and their long white beards. Rowing home, in the evenings, they sing Russian songs.

RUMÄNIEN.
KIRHANA SFÎNTU. GHEORGHE. DELTA.
1958.
Die Kirhanas sind die Kooperativen, hier werden die gefangenen
Fische abgeliefert, gewogen und zum Weitertransport verpackt.

RUMANIA.
KIRHANA SFÎNTU. GHEORGHE. 1958.
Kirhanas are co-operatives to which the catch is brought,
weighed and packed for transport.

RUMÄNIEN.
KIRHANA SFÎNTU. GHEORGHE. 1958.
Triumphierend werden die frischgefangenen Störe in den Kühlraum gerollt und auf Eis gelegt, bis das Schiff zum Weitertransport nach Tulcea ankommt.

RUMANIA.
KIRHANA SFÎNTU. GHEORGHE. 1958.
Just caught sturgeons are triumphantly rolled in to be put on ice until the boat to Tulcea arrives.

RUMÄNIEN. PASSAGIERBOOT VON GALAŢI
NACH TULCEA. 1958.

Rechts: Das Gepäck der Passagiere besteht aus Säcken und fest
mit Tüchern zugebundenen Körben; es riecht nach Käse und
Gemüse. Sie wollen zum Markt nach Tulcea, dort ist das Geschäft
gut, die Deltaboote müssen versorgt werden.

RUMANIA. PASSENGER BOAT FROM GALAŢI
TO TULCEA. 1958.

Right: The luggage of the passengers consists of sacks and
tightly covered baskets. It smells of cheese and vegetables. They
are going to the market in Tulcea, where business is good.
The Delta boats have to buy provisions.

RUMÄNIEN. SULINA. 1994.

Links: "Gute Reise", der Besitzer des Hotels Sulina verabschiedet
sich. Es ist Sonntagmorgen und mehrere Stunden sind mit der
Suche nach Benzin zugebracht worden. Auch die Zündkerzen der
Schaluppe lassen zu wünschen übrig, unser Fahrer verbringt viel
Zeit damit, auf dem Bauch liegend in den Motor zu starren und
Kontakte herzustellen. Inzwischen halten wir zwar das Steuer fest,
aber das Boot dreht sich hilflos in der von den Bugwellen großer
Frachter zerschnittenen Donau. Wir kommen im Hafen von Tulcea
gerade bei Einfall der Dunkelheit an.

RUMANIA. SULINA. 1994.

Left: "Happy journey". The owner of the Hotel Sulina waves good-
bye. It is Sunday morning and several hours have been spent trying
to find gasoline for the trip back to Tulcea. It turns out that the
spark plugs of our motor also leave a lot to be desired, the driver
spends most of his time lying belly-down next to the open hood,
trying to get them to work. Meanwhile one of us hangs onto the
stearing wheel, but the boat turns helplessly in the wake created by
a passing freighter. We manage to dock in Tulcea, just as darkness
starts to settle.

RUMÄNIEN. DAS SCHWARZE MEER AM ENDE
DES SULINA-KANALS. 1994.

Niemand weiß genau, wo die Donau wirklich ins Schwarze Meer
mündet. Sigmund von Birken aus Pegnitz nennt in seinem 1684
erschienen Werk über die Donau sieben Mündungen:

Hierostomum - Heilige Mündung

Narkostomum - Träge Mündung

Kalostomum - Schöne Mündung

Pseudostomum - Falsche Mündung

Boreostomum - Nördliche Mündung

Stenostotum - Enge Mündung

Spirostomum - Geschlängelte Mündung

RUMANIA. THE BLACK SEA NEAR THE END
OF THE SULINA CANAL. 1994.

No one knows exactly where the Danube really ends in the Black
Sea. Sigmund von Birken from Pegnitz wrote a book about the
Danube in 1684 and names seven mouths:

Hierostomum - Holy Mouth

Narcostomum - Lazy Mouth

Kalostomum - Beautiful Mouth

Pseudostomum - False Mouth

Boreostomum - Northern Mouth

Stenostomum - Narrow Mouth

Spirostomum - Winding Mouth

GEDANKEN ZU DIESEM BUCH

INGE MORATH

Mein lieber Bruder, wann
bauen wir uns ein Floß
und fahren den Himmel hinunter?

Ingeborg Bachmann 1954

I need my memories
They are my documents.

Louise Bourgeois

Wasser hat es mir schon
immer angetan.

Strömendes Wasser, Fluß-
wasser. "Schönströmend" nann-
te Hesiod die in römischen Zeiten Ister genannte Donau. So
habe ich sie vielleicht zum
ersten Mal gesehen, als Kind,
in der Wachau, auf Ferien.

Legenden haben es mir an-
getan. Donauweibchen, Ahn-
frauen von Undinen und Melu-
sinen; Nixen und Wassermän-
ner, die Schiffer in Strudel
locken; zu Felsen erstarrte
Raubritter und Wegelagerer;
die Geschichte vom Schneider,
der bei der Burg Krämpelstein
auf einem Felsen hoch über der
Donau mit seiner Ziege als
Gesellschaft wohnte, sich in

ihren Hörnern verfing, als er
sie nach einem Streit über eine
delikate Angelegenheit in den
Fluß werfen wollte. Er ging mit
ihr unter, und nun kann man
ihn an gewissen Tagen um Mit-
ternacht in ihrer Gesellschaft
meckern hören.

Und natürlich die Brautfahrt
Kriemhildens zu Etzel entlang
der Donau über Passau bis
Tulln, einem der farbigsten
Abschnitte des unergründlichen
und furchtbaren Nibelungen-
liedes.

Reisen haben es mir angetan.
Reisen, die meine Neugierde
befriedigen, wo das Fahren von
einem Ort zum anderen Aus-
kunft gibt, sich vertiefen läßt,
der Weg sich bahnt und unbe-
irrbar weitergeht bis zum Ende.

Eines Tages im Mai 1958
wurde es mir klar, daß für
mich die Donau so eine unver-
meidliche Reise war.

Der Entschluß zur Abfahrt
schien schnell genug gefaßt.
Erst langsam wurde mir klar,

wie lange ich mich auf diese
Reise wirklich vorbereitet hatte,
ohne mir dessen bewußt zu
sein. Ich denke zurück. Die
Eltern meiner Mutter waren
in der k. u. k. Monarchie in
Leibnitz und Marburg, das im
heutigen Slowenien liegt, auf-
gewachsen. Ihre Geschichten
vom friedlichen Völkergemisch,
das der Erste Weltkrieg zerstörte, von Ausweisung, neuem
Ansiedeln in Graz, veranlaßten
mich, meine Nase in ein paar
Bände von Balkangeschichte zu
stecken, die sie in ihrer Bibliothek hatten und die prachtvoll
mit Kupferstichen illustriert
waren. Byzanz entdeckte ich in
den Reproduktionen der herrli-
chen Fresken der Klöster in
Jugoslawien in der Postkarten-
sammlung einer vielgereisten
Tante. Die Mutter meines Vaters
sprach Ungarisch, sie war als
junges Mädchen dort Erzieherin
bei einer adeligen Familie
gewesen, liebte Budapest, die
Pußta, ungarische Rennpferde,
Husaren, und spielte Liszt auf
ihrem großen Flügel. Später
lernte ich Rumänisch in einem

Universitätskurs über lateini-
sche Sprachen, ich war interessiert an der lateinischen Basis
dieser Sprache mit slawischen,
griechischen und türkischen
Elementen und brachte ein
Semester an der Bukarester
Universität mit weiteren Studi-
en zu. Um Geld zu verdienen,
gab ich Deutschunterricht, über-
setzte rumänische Gedichte und
Novellen und begann, die reiche Literatur der östlichen an
die Donau grenzenden Nationalitäten kennenzulernen.

Die Donau als Fluß konkreti-
sierte sich in meinem Leben
erst, als ich gegen Ende der
vierziger Jahre nach Wien zog.
Ich ging mit Freunden in die
Lobau zum Baden, zum
Fischessen und auf verliebte
Spaziergänge.

Wir fuhren nach Hainburg,
schauten die römischen Ruinen
an, stiegen auf den Braunsberg
und blickten auf die ganz
nahen Grenzen der Tschechoslowakei und Ungarns. Wir
feierten das Ende des Zweiten
Weltkrieges und das Überleben,

aber nie wieder konnte unser
Blick ungetrübt von der Ver-
gangenheit sein. Um diese Zeit
erschien Ilse Aichingers Buch
"Die größere Hoffnung" über die
Angst, die Bedrohung und die
widerständige Hoffnung der
"Kinder mit den falschen Großeltern" - der Kinder, die nach
den 'Nürnberger Gesetzen' als
jüdisch oder halbjüdisch galten
und zu Demütigung, Verhöh-
nung und oft auch Tod verurteilt waren: die Donau-Auen, in
denen sich einige Szenen
traumhaft abspielen, sahen nie
mehr gleich aus. Ich fuhr mit
der Fähre über die Donau zum
ehemaligen Konzentrationslager
Mauthausen, weil Überleben
nicht Verharmlosung werden
durfte. Mehr und mehr konzen-
trierte sich, was mich innerlich
beschäftigte und interessierte in
den Regionen Mittel- und Ost-
europas, durch die sich die
Donau ihren Lauf bahnt.

Meine Arbeit als Fotografin
hatte mich schon ein paar Jahre
lang in andere Kontinente
geführt. Ich hatte gelernt, mich

auf große Fotoessays vorzubereiten: eine Fotografie entsteht in einem Augenblick, aber die plötzliche Entdeckung kann das Resultat einer langen Bekanntschaft sein. Ich wußte, daß eine Reise entlang der Donau von Anfang zum Ende weniger durch die damals noch beachtlichen Schwierigkeiten mit Transportmitteln als mit Behörden geplagt sein würde. Nicht weniger als sechs Länder mit kommunistischen Regierungen grenzten an die Donau: Tschechoslowakei, Ungarn, Jugoslawien, Bulgarien, Rumänien und die Sowjetunion (Ukraine). Alle hatten exquisit komplizierte Spielregeln für Journalisten und Fotografen, die dort arbeiten wollten, ausgetüftelt: Entweder bekam man ohnehin kein Visa, oder nur zur Durchreise, oder für ein bis drei Tage Aufenthalt mit dem vagen Hinweis, daß man, einmal im Lande, vielleicht mehr Glück mit den lokalen Behörden hätte. Sicher war nichts. Die verschiedenen staatlichen Touristenorganisationen waren allmächtig und ließen sich, auch für die Tage, die mit Warten auf Permits vergeudet wurden, volle Tarife bezahlt.

Wie werde ich diesen Fluß fotografieren? Auf dem Weg zur Quelle nach Donaueschingen im

gemieteten Volkswagen befiel mich eine gewisse Panik. Auf wieviel Arten kann man Wasser fotografieren, was kann man damit mitteilen? Dann beruhigte ich mich wieder: Flüsse sind nicht nur Wasser, sie haben eine Geschichte, von Generationen von Menschen auf ihren Ufern geschrieben. Allmählich fand ich, was ich tun konnte: mit der Kamera über die große Vielfalt des Flusses zu berichten, über die Mannigfaltigkeit der sich überlagernden Schichten von Zivilisationen, die dieser Wasserlauf trennt und vereinigt. Bilder würden nie alles zu berichten in der Lage sein, aber das Ganze könnte einer Liebeserklärung nahe kommen: der Bitte an das Objekt meiner Zuneigung, meinem dringenden Wunsch nach Erkenntnis seines Wesens nachzugeben.

Aus der ersten Reise wurden viele Reisen, kurz oder lang, je nach den Launen der Regimes und meinen pekuniären Verhältnissen. Ich war hartnäckig, wenn man mich an einem Ort nicht reinließ, versuchte ich's anderswo, wenn ich kein Geld hatte, nahm ich Kredit auf. Es hat sich gelohnt, der langsame Weg hat mich bereichert, tausend Neugierden

befriedigt und aufgeweckt. Die benutzten Transportarten waren vielfältig: ich ging zu Fuß, chauffierte, machte Lasterstop, nahm Züge, Kähne, Fähren und Dampfer. Aus Flugzeugen durfte man leider nicht fotografieren, in den fünfziger Jahren flogen sie niedrig und die Landschaften formten Reliefs wie phantastische Landkarten.

Die Reisen folgten den Windungen des Wasserlaufs, manchmal wichen sie vom Fluß ab, auf den Spuren von Menschen und Armeen, die sich auf ihm in neue, unbekannte Länder hatten tragen lassen. Ich habe eine Menge verschiedener Essen gegessen, weich und hart, und gar nicht geschlafen; vor allem haben mir Menschen ihre Geschichten erzählt, sie ließen mich fotografieren und oft halfen ihre Lebenserfahrungen zu besserem Verständnis.

Man muß zielbewußt durch die Türe gehen, aber man soll sie offen lassen. Die Dinge um uns sind immer da, aber wir müssen sie entdecken: diesen Baum in diesem Licht, diese Landschaft von diesem Hügel, diese Hand mit dem Stück Papier, das ihr so wichtig ist; diese Donau und ihre Menschen mit ihren Leiden, Freu-

den und Kämpfen, verstrickt in die Konsequenzen ihrer Geschichte. Die Augen weit offen zu halten ist vielleicht eine Weise, vieles das uns als entfernt und überholt erscheint, als lebendige Gegenwart zu erfahren.

Der erste Donauessay wurde 1959 von der Zeitschrift Paris Match und später von anderen internationalen Zeitschriften veröffentlicht. Ich wußte, daß er keineswegs komplett war, und kehrte immer wieder an die Donau zurück, um zu fotografieren. 1993 boten mir die Galerie Fotohof und der Otto Müller Verlag an, die Reise noch einmal zu unternehmen und schließlich aus allen Reisen ein Buch zu machen. Ich habe natürlich nicht einen Moment gezögert. Die letzten Fotos wurden im Frühjahr 1995 aufgenommen, unlogischerweise an der Quelle. Hölderlin liebte die Idee, daß die Donau im umgekehrten Sinne verlaufe: vom Schwarzen Meer in den deutschen Schwarzwald, die griechische Helle in den dunklen Norden tragend. Seltsam ist auch, daß die Länge dieses Flusses nicht ab der Quelle, sondern ab seiner Mündung berechnet wird, der Kilometerstein 0 steht im Schwarzen-Meer-Hafen von Sulina.

MUSINGS ABOUT THIS BOOK

INGE MORATH

Mein lieber Bruder,
wann bauen wir uns ein Floß
und fahren den Himmel hinunter?
     Ingeborg Bachmann 1954

I need my memories
They are my documents.
     Louise Bourgeois

I always loved water. Flowing water, the water of rivers. Hesios wrote that the Ister - as the Danube was called by the Romans - was "beautiful(ly)streaming", and that's probably how I saw the river first, as a child on vacation in the Wachau region.

I love legends: the Danube-nayads, ancestresses of Ondines and Melusines; nymphs and water sprites seducing sailors into watery deaths, robber knights turned into rocky columns, the story of the taylor who lived by the Castle of Krämpelstein on top of a steep rock high above the Danube. He got caught on the horns of his goat as he tried to throw it into the river after a quarrel about a delicate matter and occasionally now, at the stroke of midnight, can be heard bleating in its company.

And above all, the voyage of Kriemhild along the Danube past Passau to Tulln on her way to meet her future husband Etzel, one of the most colourful passages in the unfathomable and terrible Song of the Nibelungs.

I love voyages. Voyages that satisfy curiosity, where the going from one place to the other informs, allows one to go deeper, following a path without hesitation, unable to stray until one sees the end.

One day, in May of the year 1958, it became clear to me that to follow the Danube from its source to its end was, in my mind, one of those inevitable voyages.

The decision to set off seemed to happen swiftly, and it gradually dawned on me, how long I had prepared myself for this trip without being conscious of it. I try to think back: My mother's parents lived in the part of the Austro-Hungarian Empire that now belongs to Slovenia. Their tales of a peaceful multinational co-existence shattered by the First World War; then of their being expelled to resettle in Graz, Austria, made me stick my nose into a couple of splendidly illustrated volumes of The History of the Balkans which they had in their library. I discovered the Byzantine culture in reproductions of the marvellous frescoes of Yugoslav monasteries in the postcard collection of an aunt addicted to visiting these places. My father's mother spoke Hungarian, for as a young woman she had been a governess in a grand Hungarian household. She adored Budapest, the Puszta, Hungarian racehorses and hussars, and played Liszt romantically on her grand piano. Later, in the university, I enrolled in a course of Latin languages. Rumanian I found especially interesting with its Latin base below the Slav, Greek and Turkish overlays. I spent a semester in Bucharest to further my studies, earning money by giving German language lessons and translating Rumanian poetry and short stories into German, thus starting an aquaintanceship with the rich literature of the peoples living in the countries bordering on the eastern part of the Danube.

As a river, the Danube only really entered my life when I moved to Vienna towards the end of the Forties. With friends I went to the Lobau to swim and eat fish, and took romantic walks. We went to Hainburg to look at the Roman ruins and climbed up a mountain, called the Braunsberg, from which we could see the borders of three countries, Austria, Czechoslovakia (now Slovakia) and Hungary. We celebrated the end of the Second World War and our survival, but were unable to ever again be untroubled by the past. At that time a book entitled "The Greater Hope" by the young poet Ilse Aichinger appeared. It dealt with the fears, the menaces and the resistant hope of the children, who, according to the Nazi "Nuremberg Laws", were condemned to suffer persecution and derision and finally death. The water-meadows around the Danube near Vienna, in which some of the dreamlike scenes of the past took place, never again looked the same. I took the ferry across the Danube to the former concentration camp of Mauthausen; it was a devastating experience, but survival should never be allowed to render the past harmless. More and more, for these and other reasons, my inner preoccupations and interests seemed to be concentrated in the regions of Central and Eastern Europe through which the Danube makes its way.

My work as a photographer had taken me, since 1953, to a number of continents. I had learned to prepare myself for big photographic essays. A photograph is made in a fraction of a second, but the sudden discovery can well be the fruit of long aquaintance. I knew that a trip along the Danube in 1958 would not be plagued as much by difficulties with transport, a big problem in those days, as by totalitarian bureaucracy.

No less than six states with communist governments bordered the river: Hungary, Yugoslavia, Bulgaria, Rumania and the USSR (Ukraine). All of them had developed exquisitely Byzantine rules for visiting journalists or photographers. Either one was refused a visa right away; or one got one only good for transit; or for a stay of one to three days, but with restrictions as to the places one could visit. Occasionally, a hint was dropped that, once in the

country, one might be able to make better arrangements, but this was never sure. The government travel agencies were all-powerful and made one pay full tariff even for the days wasted waiting around for permits.

"How will I photograph this river?" On the road to the source of the Danube in Donaueschingen I was suddenly overcome by panic. In how many ways can one photograph water, and what can such pictures convey? Then I calmed down: a river is more than water, a river has a history written on its banks by generations of people who, in effect, have left us their stories there.

Gradually, I found what I could do - capture some of the Danube's infinite variety, the layers of its civilisations which this lovely band of water unites and divides. Pictures could never be the whole story, but could be like a declaration of love: Ask the object of your

desire to yield to your wish to get to know it wholly.

The first trip turned into many trips. Shorter and longer ones, depending on bureaucratic whims and my pecuniary situation. I was stubborn, if they did not let me in one place, I tried another, if I had no money, I borrowed it. It was worth it; the unhurried voyage has enriched me, awakening or putting to rest a thousand questions. As to means of transport, I have had to try a number of them. I went on foot, drove cars, hitched truck rides, rode trains, ferries, boats and steamers. Unfortunately, it was totally forbidden to take pictures out of planes which flew very low at the time, but gave one a view of landscapes in splendid relief.

No trip went in a straight line. I followed the meanderings of the waterway, deviated to the right or left, following the roads taken by

people and armies on the way to new, unconquered territories.

I ate many kinds of different foods, slept on hard or soft mattresses or not at all. Above all, I met people and listened to their stories and they let me photograph them and offered me some of their life experiences, which sometimes opened me to new and better understanding.

One has to go through the door, but must leave it open. The things that surround us are always there, the task is to discover them: this tree in this light, this landscape from this hill, this hand holding an all-important piece of paper; this river Danube, its people with their joys and sufferings, enmeshed in the consequences of its history. Seeing sharply may be a way to experience, as vibrant and very immediate truth, much that seems remote and outdated.

The first Danube Essay was published in 1959 in the French

magazine Paris Match and subsequently in a number of other international magazines. I knew it was far from complete and returned to photograph places along the Danube over the course of years. In 1993 the opportunity to revisit the river Danube down its entire length and gather the work into a book, was offered to me by the Galerie Fotohof with Salzburg's Otto Müller publishing house.

I did not hesitate for a moment. The last pictures in this book were shot in 1995, ending up, oddly enough, at the source. Hölderlin liked the idea of the Danube running backwards, from the Black Sea to the Black Forest, bringing Greek enlightenment to the dark North. It also seems strange that the length of this river is counted not from the source, but from the Delta where it ends at the Black Sea port of Sulina; there the measuring marker "0" stands.